YOU'RE IN CHARGE!

Writing to Communicate

Gro Frydenberg

Cynthia A. Boardman

University of California Extension, Irvine

Addison-Wesley Publishing Company

A Publication of the World Language Division

Editorial: Kathleen Sands Boehmer

Production/Manufacturing: James W. Gibbons

Design: ZBR Publications

Cover Design: Bonnie McGrath

Cover Photograph: Jim McGrath

Photo Credits: p. 16, Agustin Estrada; p. 109, courtesy of Gro Frydenberg; p. 124, copyright A&M Records, Inc. Used by permission. All rights reserved; p. 125, David Nutter.

Library of Congress Cataloging-in-Publication Data

Frydenberg, Gro.
    You're in Charge: Writing to Communicate / Gro Frydenberg.
Cynthia Boardman.
        p.   cm.
    Includes index.
    ISBN 0-201-50350-6
    1. English language—Textbooks for foreign speakers. 2. English language—Rhetoric. I. Boardman, Cynthia. II. Title.
PE1128.F76 1990 ·   89-6684
808'.042—dc20   CIP

ISBN: 0-201-50350-6
        15 16 17 18 19 20 - CRS - 98 97 96

To
Grete and Reidar Frydenberg
and
Madelyne and Dan Boardman

CONTENTS

PART II: THE ESSAY

PART III: RHETORICAL PATTERNS

To the Teacher

This writing text is intended for the ESL student who has had previous experience with the writing of paragraph length compositions and some exposure to the rhetorical structure of a written paragraph. These are students who usually have TOEFL scores in the 450—500 range; however, we have also had experience with students above this range who still have benefited from the materials as their organizational abilities have not been sufficiently solid.

This book is divided into three parts. The first part deals with paragraph organization and the paragraph characteristics of coherence, cohesion, unity, and completeness. The second part makes the transition from paragraph to full-length essay. The third part discusses in detail certain simple rhetorical patterns. These are process, classification, comparison and contrast, and exemplification.

The transition from having been expected to produce writing which only showed evidence of some thinking ability and reasonable grammatical accuracy to writing intentionally structured paragraphs and essays is a very difficult one for most students. For this reason, we have included the lengthy middle section with extensive practice in writing the central three components of an academic essay: the introductory paragraph, the essay body, and the conclusion. This is an important section for the students to develop a feeling of mastering the art of essay writing and for them to succeed in doing the work of the following section.

To complete all of the exercises, discussions, and group projects in this book would, we estimate, require a minimum of 60 hours (for example 12 weeks, 5 days a week) of classroom time devoted only to the teaching of writing. While some programs do set aside that amount of time, others do not, and the instructor of the writing course must choose which exercises to work on and which to skip. Depending on the class level, the first section may be review to such an extent that only some of the work may be deemed necessary, while for others less thorough work on rhetorical essay patterns may be more appropriate. The text is designed in such a way that the instructor can select those exercises that are most relevant for his or her class. However, the teacher should be aware that the models are structured so as to be progressively more complicated linguistically throughout the book. For this reason, we would recommend keeping to the basic chapter order. In addition, it should be noted that the first ten chapters of the book are equal in terms of class time to the last four chapters.

We believe that the creation of good writing products, be they essays, novels, poems, or plays, is a recursive process requiring repeated steps of thinking, organizing, rethinking, writing, rewriting, etc. For this reason, this book contains a large number of prewriting exercises, both group and individual. These are intended to motivate students and to help them along the path from idea to essay.

In addition, we have included a Paragraph Checklist or a Peer Help Worksheet at the end of almost every chapter. The Paragraph Checklists are designed to focus the students' attention on their own paragraphs and on how they are doing at incorporating the points of a particular chapter into their own writing. In Part II, we initiate the Peer Help Worksheets, which have the aim of aiding the students in the process of editing and revising their writing with the help of a classmate and to remind them that they are not writing for an audience of a particular teacher but for an imagined "general audience." We believe that self-evaluation, as well as group and peer work are essential to support the students in their quest for emancipation from their previous dependence on the teacher.

TEACHING SUGGESTIONS

Most of the chapters in this book begin with one or more models of the type of writing the students will be asked to do. These models are intended to be used inductively as starting points for discussion of the types of organizational patterns used for different purposes. Frequently, studying the models and the following explanations may best be assigned as homework prior to the first class dealing with that chapter.

The exercises are of various types: analysis, short-answer, discussion, and production. The primary emphasis of the text is on the latter two types. Whenever the text consists of explanations of the models or of other points, these are included for students to have in writing what the teacher has already explained or described orally.

There are as many ways to use a textbook as there are students and instructors with their special needs and styles. However, we would like to give some general suggestions based on two chapters to describe methods which have been successful in the past use of these materials.

Part I, Chapter 3

Day 1 (50 min.)

1. Reiterate that not all paragraphs in academic English are structured as the models, but that it is a common organizational pattern.

2. Write: TOPIC SENTENCE = TOPIC + CONTROLLING IDEA on the board. Draw the students' attention to the model paragraph and have them decide what the topic and controlling idea of that sentence are. (Topic: first day in Yugoslavia, controlling idea: worst day)

3. Ask the students to write down in note-form the examples given that show this day as "the worst day." Do these examples convince you that it really was an awful day? If they do, then they support the TS. This is the BODY of the paragraph.

4. Write the nine examples of topic sentences in this chapter on the board or on a transparency. Explain the differences between them.

5. Have the students do EXERCISE 1 in pairs and check the answers.

6. Divide the class into small groups. There are many ways of doing this. You can focus on mixing speakers of different native languages, learning styles, or personalities, or you can randomize the grouping by handing out cards with different colors in no particular order and tell them to find the others with the same color cards. EXERCISE 2 is a production exercise with no "right" answers. The purpose of the exercise is to have students practice approaching a topic in different ways depending on the purpose of writing. After they have written as many topic sentences as they can, two groups may join to compare results and to discuss whether their sentences qualify as topic sentences.

Homework could consist of doing EXERCISE 3.

Day 2 (50 min.)

The authors believe that students in a writing class should be spending the bulk of their time discussing, thinking, organizing, writing, revising, editing, and writing again. For this reason, we recommend that the instructor limit the amount of time that he or she use in explanation, and that lessons be structured inductively instead. This means that students should search for and discuss the structure of the many model paragraphs and essays rather than have their structure pointed out to them.

1. Have students write their topic sentences from Exercise 3 on three transparencies and show these on an overhead projector. Discuss the differences, making sure to point out all the positive aspects of the students' suggestions.

2. Section B shows three common ways to support topic sentences. Ask the students to number the facts/statistics and examples given in the first two models, and, secondly, discuss how the third model paragraph differs from the second.

3. Ask the students to read the two models in Section C and to underline the topic and concluding sentences in each. How are they different?

4. At this point, it's time to compose a paragraph. Ask the students to complete the writing assignment in Section D. To make sure that they follow the suggested procedure, you may wish to give a writing timetable, such as:

    5 min. brainstorming/freewriting

    5 min. outlining

    20 min. writing

Collect the paragraphs but do not evaluate or correct them.

Day 3 (50 min.)

1. Start with a pep talk on rewriting. Actually reading what one has written and rewriting it is often considered a tedious, teacher-enforced, and mechanical activity in many writing programs. With enthusiastic coaching, it should become as natural as writing in the first place.

2. Explain the "rewriting = revising + editing" concept.

3. You may choose to reproduce the sample paragraph with notes for revision on a transparency so that the class can discuss possible changes to make. After this, direct the students' attention to the revised paragraph to see if it matches their ideas for changes. Make sure to emphasize that this is only one possible way to revise it and that their suggestions may be equally valid.

4. This is an appropriate time to turn to the editing symbols in Appendix 4 if you have not gone over this previously. We have found that several repetitions of the meaning of the symbols throughout the course are necessary for students to get used to them.

5. Distribute yesterday's paragraphs to their writers and a partner. A pairing of students at approximately the same level of writing sophistication seems useful for this activity. Explain the peer editing assignment (Section F), and ask them to read, make notes, and discuss each others' paragraphs. Expect some initial resistance to this: students often need considerable encouragement to accept the value of comments made by anyone other than the teacher. Make sure to remind them that they, of course, are the final judges on what and how to put down in writing what they want to say. The actual rewriting can be done as homework.

PART III, CHAPTER 11

Prior to Day 1, assign the two models as homework. Ask them to think about what the *purpose* of writing essays such as these could be, who the intended *audience* might be, and how the essays are *structured*.

Day 1 (50 min.)

Bring the materials needed for the "Light Experiment" essay to class. Either bring in materials for EXERCISE 2, or (in class) ask the students to supply their own "materials."

1. Discuss in small groups the purpose, audience, and structure of the models.

2. Ask for three volunteers. Have one student give the directions for the light experiment, one conduct it, and one be the helper. Ask if there is anything they would like to add to the essay to make it clearer. (Every essay can be revised!)

3. Discuss answers to EXERCISE 1.

4. Have the students do EXERCISE 2 in pairs following the instructions.

5. You may want to copy the chronological linking words in the table from Section B to a transparency and conduct a review of the syntax used with the different types of linking words by having the students work inductively from the list of sentences from model 1.

6. Finally, ask the students to complete EXERCISE 3 and compare answers. You may also ask them to add a topic sentence to this exercise and write it as a complete paragraph.

EXERCISE 4 may be assigned as follow-up homework.

Day 2 (50 min.)

1. Start the day with work on fragments (Section C). You may want to refer the students to Appendix 1: Punctuation for an overview of punctuation rules covered in this text.

2. If you feel that your students could use a review of the concept of coherence, assign Section D as pair work. This type of exercise can also be done as a "strip story," where you (or the students) write out the sentences separately on a sheet of paper, make enough copies to have one per pair, cut the sentences apart, and scramble them. The objective is the same: reorder the sentences, but this method has the advantage of involving the students physically in the ordering process.

3. If you have the time, you may want to add other process-oriented exercises. Three suggestions are given below.

   a. *Learning by doing*

   Each student is handed a slip of paper with sentences describing a process. Their job is to explain what to do orally to the others using chronological transitions without mentioning what the point of the process is. The class guesses what is being explained.

   e.g.

   how to make a long-distance telephone call
   how to use a microwave oven
   how to shop for shoes
   how to start a motorcycle
   how to apply to a college
   how to use a jumprope
   how to play dominoes (or another game)

   b. *Show and tell*

   Bring in lots of different materials for making different things. You then proceed to give an oral process speech, doing what you are describing.

   e.g.

   making a Valentine's Day card (or any card)
   making potato prints
   making origami birds
   dying Easter eggs etc.

   (Make sure you structure your speech by first listing the materials needed—show them while you describe them—then go on to a step by step description of the process and the product.)

   The students then choose different materials to make something of their own and describe the process to each other in small groups. These "speeches" should be informal and impromptu.

c. *Round-robin writing*

Students sit in circles of five (or however many works for your class). Each student is handed a large sheet of paper on which is written the first step in making something. Each activity should be comprised of six steps (if there are five people per group). All of them write (at the same time) a sentence which describes the next step in the process. Note: transitions are essential.

The results are read aloud. Are any steps missing?

Day 3 (50 min.)

This is the first-draft writing day. There are two choices of topics in the text. Explain the two topics and what they involve. Ask each student to choose which topic he/she would like to write. At this point in the course, the students should be so familiar with the process of brainstorming and outlining that very little teacher prompting is needed. Ask them to work in small groups, and set a time limit for the steps, e.g.:

10 min. discussion/brainstorming
10 min. group/individual outlining
30 min. first draft writing

Collect the first drafts, but do not correct or grade them.

Day 4 (50 min.)

The students have had some previous experience with paragraph checklists as well as exposure to Peer Help Worksheets. We suggest that you reiterate that we can all help each other become better writers and that writing is an interaction between a writer and his/her audience. Both the writer and the helper gain from reading each other's essays since both develop their insight into the process of composing a written product.

1. After you have given the "pep talk," pair up students and return the first drafts to their writers. You may want to choose a different method of pairing students each time, e.g. different native languages, a highly structured but boring essay with an unorganized but interesting one, or simply pairing writers who normally do not interact much. Ask them to read each other's essay and fill in the Peer Help Worksheet. Give a time limit, e.g. 15 minutes.

2. Ask the students to return the essays to their writers along with the worksheet. Give them a time limit of 15-20 minutes to discuss improvements in the two essays.

3. You may choose to have the students revise their essays in class or as homework. If you have noticed common problems in your reading of their first drafts, this is the time to go over those areas.

Homework: Ask the students to bring to class any written or pictorial "how to" materials they have at home, such as instructions accompanying any piece of electronic equipment (VCR, camera, etc.), cookbooks, college catalogs (how to apply), or a box of detergent. They will quickly discover that there are process instructions all around them.

Day 5 (50 min.)

1. As a corollary to writing about processes, there are several grammatical structures which should be reviewed. You may want to go over the use of imperatives and reduced adverb clauses, in particular.

2. Ask the students to show what they have brought and explain the instructions. Review vocabulary and structure.

3. At this point, the class should start thinking about topics for the week's home essay. The topics in Section G of the text can be used as points of departure. Depending on the interests of your particular class, you may suggest others, for example, topics taken from individual students" interest areas or college majors. Remind them that a process can be as general as "How to live a happy life" or as specific as "How to start a manual transmission car." Ask them to discuss possible topics for their essays in small groups. Then give them 10 minutes to freewrite about their individual topics.

Homework: Ask the students to read the two models from Chapter 12, looking for the same aspects as in the models in Chapter 11.

* * * * * * * * * * *

There are as many ways of using a textbook as there are instructors and learners. We hope that the above suggestions will help you in developing a writing course that both you and your students will find educational as well as enjoyable.

ACKNOWLEDGEMENTS

We would like to acknowledge the Program in English as a Second Language at the University of California Extension, Irvine, in general and, in particular, those teachers who used the drafts in their classes and who gave us important feedback. Special thanks are owed to Sheila Goff and Bill Rindfleisch for taking the time to give us a detailed commentary of our first draft.

We would also like to thank the reviewers of this book, Jill Brand, Center for English Language and Orientation Programs at Boston University; Liz England, English as a Second Language, Eastern Michigan University; Catherine Sadow, Northeastern University, whose suggestions helped us tremendously in the rewriting process.

We are also indebted to Jerry Bower for sharing his word processing expertise with us.

Finally, we wish to thank Kathleen Sands-Boehmer and Addison-Wesley for their constant support of the project from its beginning through many ups and downs.

To the Student

This textbook is designed to help you become a better writer of American English. It will teach you about the process of writing. This process consists of more than just writing from the beginning to the end of a composition. Writing is a process because it goes through many stages. It starts with thinking, planning, and organizing. The next steps involve writing and rewriting. To be a good writer is to constantly change and improve what you have already written.

The major focus of this book is the organization of academic essays. You will find that the American approach to writing is very direct. This style of organization may or may not be the kind that you use in your native language. It is important to note here that how a piece of writing is organized can vary from language to language. This is not to say that the organization of one is better than it is in another, only that it may be different.

To become a better writer, you must start somewhere, and that place is to learn the basics of format and formulation. Once these basics are under control (a process that will take a while), there is room for variation and innovation.

In addition to organization, you will learn other aspects of writing conventions, including punctuation, the use of linking words, and paragraph and essay format. Furthermore, we hope you will have a bit of fun with the prewriting activities and writing assignments. They are designed to help you find original content for your writing by stimulating your own thinking.

PART I

The Paragraph

1 Introduction to Academic Writing

A. WHY DO YOU WRITE?

At American colleges and universities, students are asked to write for several different reasons. Some of these purposes of writing are listed below:

to report on a laboratory experiment
to compare two theories/scientists/concepts
to argue for a solution to a problem
to describe a project that the student has worked on
to summarize what other experts have said

The students are asked to use these purposes in a variety of academic situations, such as in composition classes, and for essay tests, term papers, laboratory reports, and project reports.

B. HOW DO YOU WRITE?

In all of these writing situations, the students have to use a certain format and style of writing. Every student is expected to write clearly and simply with good grammar and correct spelling, but, in addition, writing at American colleges and universties follows a certain basic format which is important to learn. The two main formats (or organizations) of writing are the PARAGRAPH and the ESSAY. Paragraph format is used to answer test questions and also often in laboratory reports. The paragraph format is also used as one part of the essay. Essay format is used in compositions, term papers, research papers, and so on.

The STYLE of writing is also important. Students in the United States are expected to write in a somewhat formal, but not heavily formal style. This means that their language should be clear and direct and that they should not use slang in their academic writing. In addition, it is important to note that students in the United States are often expected to use their own ideas in their writing. American professors consider original examples and arguments to be more valuable than just a repetition of what other people have said.

Students at American universities often have very little time to do their writing. They may, for example, have a test requiring several paragraph answers in a short period of time. When your time is limited, it becomes extra important not to waste any of it wondering how to say what you want to say. In addition, basic American organizational format is often quite different from the way writing is organized in other countries. For these reasons, in this book you will study how American academic writing is organized, and you will write and rewrite lots of paragraphs and essays. Keep in mind that the only way to improve is to practice!

C. TO WHOM DO YOU WRITE?

Since the ultimate purpose of writing is communication, any writer needs to be aware of whom he/she is writing to. This person or people are called the audience. For writers of textbooks, the audience consists of students. For business people, the audience may be a colleague or an employer (in the case of memos and reports), or it may be a potential customer (in letters and promotions). For novelists, the audience is the general public.

The question here is who is the audience for students? In the short run, the audience may be a classmate or classmates, and in the long run, the audience is the students' teacher or professor. However, the purpose of writing is still the same: to communicate a message. The business person and the student may have different styles and content in their writing, but they both need to be aware of their audience, and they both must deal with the problems in making a message clear. Those problems of clarity, organization, and even punctuation are the same for both writers.

Therefore, as you write to complete assignments as students, keep in mind the classmate or the teacher to whom you are writing, but remember that what you learn will help you with the writing in English you may do at any point in your life.

D. YOU'RE IN CHARGE: WRITING TO COMMUNICATE

Below you will find five common academic writing situations. Pick one of them and write a paragraph about it.

Topic 1

You are a student in an art class. Your professor has asked you to describe a member of your family in detail, so that the other students can draw a picture from your description. Consider the person's age, size, hair, face, and anything else that can help the other students form a picture in their minds of that person.

Topic 2

You are a student in a journalism class. Your assignment is to report on an accident that you have seen or that you have been involved in. Since you can't possibly write about everything that happened, make sure you pick out the major details. Every newspaper story should answer the questions:

Who was involved?
What happened?
Where did it take place?
When did it happen?
Why did it occur?

Topic 3

You are taking a world history class. The students in your class come from many different countries, and they are not very familiar with the history of yours. As part of a class project, your instructor has asked all of you to write a paragraph about the life of an important person in your country's history.

Topic 4

You are taking a sociology class, and you are studying how different lifestyles influence different ways of thinking. Your assignment is to compare the way your mother or father lived when she or he was your age with the way you live now. Is your life now different from or similar to the way your mother/father lived?

Topic 5

You are a student of architecture. Your class is studying what different people really want in a house. Your assignment is to describe your dream house in as much detail as possible. Think about what your dream house shows about your personality and the way you want to live. Consider such things as its size, building materials, number of rooms, types of rooms, furniture, garden, etc.

2 Types of Paragraphs

Paragraphs are organized differently depending on what the purpose is for writing them. There are three main kinds of paragraphs in English, and each kind is organized according to its purpose.

A. NARRATIVE PARAGRAPHS

A NARRATIVE paragraph tells a story. Look at this example.

Example 1   My first full day in Yugoslavia turned out to be my worst day there. I woke up late in my small hotel room. I wanted to take a quick shower, but there was no hot water. In fact, there was only ice cold water. I went down to breakfast and was served a stale roll and lukewarm tea. Next, I got lost trying to find my way to the meeting that I was already late for. I couldn't find anyone who spoke English, and my Croatian was still not very good. At last, I found the meeting place, but I also found out that the meeting had been postponed to the following day. I got lost again on my way back to the hotel and spent most of the day "sightseeing" on various city buses. Finally, I arrived back at the hotel ready for dinner. The waiter politely told me that I was too late for dinner. I went up to my room tired and hungry. Little did I know that this would be → future my worst day, so I had nothing but good days to look forward to.

VOCABULARY
stale = not fresh
lukewarm = between hot and cold
"sightseeing" = the quotation marks ('' '') around this word shows that it is not used in its ordinary meaning
Croatian = one of the languages spoken in Yugoslavia

This is a story about one day. You can, of course, tell stories of shorter or greater length. The important thing in a narrative paragraph is that you tell a story.

An observation report is another example of a narrative paragraph. Read the one below.

Example 2   I learned a lot about planning and organizing a Kindergarten class during my observation day at Matell Park Elementary School on November 22nd. At 8:00 AM, Mrs. Anderson, the teacher, welcomed me and proudly showed me her room. Before the students arrived, I helped Mrs. Anderson arrange the low tables and chairs for that day's groups. At 8:15, she opened the door and let the 30 five-year olds inside. They quietly put their backpacks away and went to sit down in a circle. Then Mrs. Anderson greeted each one by name and asked them what day, date, and month it was. After this, they all counted together how many days they had been in school so far. Next, she called out the names of students who should go to different colored tables. At this point, her aide arrived and started helping one group with an assignment in tracing letters. Each group of five children had a different job to do. After group time, they all went to the computer room, where they practiced drawing shapes on the computer screen. The next activity was music time, and the children clapped their hands and sang a few songs. Following this, they went outside for a snack while Mrs. Anderson and I set up the room for art. When the children came back in, they were allowed to choose which art activity they wanted to do, and they went to the tables they had chosen. The final part of the day was story time, when Mrs. Anderson read two stories. Because of her excellent organization of both the room and her time, Mrs. Anderson taught me that 30 children can indeed learn something, cooperate, behave politely, and enjoy themselves at the same time.

VOCABULARY

insight = understanding
a backpack = a bag that you carry on your back
an aide = a classroom helper
to trace = to write on top of something else

B. DESCRIPTIVE PARAGRAPHS

The second kind of paragraph is a DESCRIPTIVE paragraph. This kind of paragraph is used when you need to describe what something looks like in a physical way. You might need to describe a city in an essay about life abroad, the equipment for a report on a laboratory experiment, or how a person looks for an essay about that person. Here are two examples.

Example 1   The child's face reflected her cheerful and determined nature. Her hair was bright red and had a royal blue bow tied at the top. The skin on her forehead, as well as her entire face, was soft white and covered with freckles. Her eyes were a sparkling blue and, at that moment, were focused on the end of her turned up nose. Her lips were a natural red and slightly parted. Coming from between these lips was a tongue stretching to its limit in an upward direction. In short, she looked determined to touch her tongue to her nose, perhaps simply to prove to herself that it could be done.

VOCABULARY

bright red = a strong red color
royal blue = a strong, medium blue color
parted lips = a little open

Example 2   The sleepy little harbor town of Chania gave me a feeling of total peace. On this Sunday morning, it was deserted. From my window overlooking the port, I could see a freighter off in the distance. On my right the sun was streaming in through the white lace curtains fluttering in the early morning breeze. At this time of the day, it was still a friendly sun, bright and cheerful with the promise of simple pleasures. It shone on the wooden boats pulled up on the beach below and made their colors of pink, purple, green, and yellow stand out in contrast to the white sand. On my left, the harbor road curved around to the lighthouse at the tip of the peninsula. Not a car could be seen, and no sounds of engines broke the stillness of the morning. The merchants had not yet opened their ocean-blue shutters, and the chairs of the cafes were still stacked on top of the tables with their legs pointing up to the endless sky. I had a feeling of being in complete harmony with the world around me.

VOCABULARY
a port = harbor
a freighter = a ship which carries goods, not people
a peninsula = a piece of land sticking out into the water like a finger
shutters = wooden window-coverings

The descriptions allow the reader to get a mental picture of what the little girl or the city of Chania looked like at one particular time. This is the goal of a descriptive paragraph.

C. EXPOSITORY PARAGRAPHS

In addition to the above, there are several other purposes for writing academic paragraphs and essays. Some of these are:

1. to compare two things (buildings, computers, economic theories, etc.)

2. to show the steps in a process (how to increase profits, how to evaluate a painting, etc.)

3. to analyze something
   a) dividing something into its parts (different theories of learning, different kinds of governments, people, etc.)
   b) analyzing a problem (air pollution, nuclear power, the wars in the Middle East, etc.)

4. to persuade
   a) to make others do something (vote for someone, sign a petition, join an organization, etc.)
   b) to argue for your personal opinion (freeway traffic, American cars, the tax laws, grades in school, etc.)

All these purposes lead to what we call EXPOSITORY writing. They try to explain something to the reader. Read the following example.

Example 1   A personal computer consists of three main components which have different functions. The first is the central processing unit, or CPU. This is the brain of the computer. This unit contains the memory of the machine and the microchips which make the computer able to perform its functions. The CPU has one or more disk drives, where we can put program diskettes to make the machine add numbers, do word processing, or play games. The second component is the monitor. This looks much like a small TV, but of course it doesn't have any channel buttons. On the monitor screen we can observe what we are telling the computer to do, such as move words, draw figures, or shoot down space aliens. The third component is the keyboard. It has the shape of a typewriter keyboard with letters and numbers, but, in addition, it also contains specialized keys for computing: function keys, cursor movement arrows, and command keys. We use the keyboard to input letters, numbers, and commands to the computer. With a CPU, a monitor, and a keyboard, we have a complete computer.

— repeat focus.

VOCABULARY

a component = a part
a function = a use
to perform = to do
word processing = writing and editing
a cursor = a blinking square or line which shows you where you are in the text
to input = to send data to the machine

This paragraph explains the parts of a computer. Therefore, it is an expository paragraph. Another expository paragraph follows. It explains how the space shuttle can be reused.

Example 2　　　The space shuttle can be used again and again. When it takes off, it is attached to a rocket which has three main engines plus two booster engines. These engines are separated from the rocket after their fuel is used up. After eight minutes of flight, the shuttle gets rid of its main liquid fuel tank. At this point, the space shuttle enters earth orbit. In order to return to the ground, it fires two small extra engines backwards to reduce speed and lands like an airplane on a runway. It is then given a piggy-back ride on a 747 jet back to the place where it was launched to be refitted with new booster engines and a new fuel tank. After it is checked carefully, the space shuttle can take another trip into space.

VOCABULARY

a booster engine = an extra, helping engine
orbit = a circle around a planet
piggy-back = attached to the back of something else
to launch = to shoot up a rocket

Exercise 1

Identify each of the following paragraphs as narrative (N), descriptive (D) or expository (E). Circle the correct letter.

1.   The old bookcase was very cluttered. On the top shelf, there were two plants. Both appeared to be dying due to a lack of water. The second shelf had a row of old, dusty books. In front of these books were little souvenirs of various places around the world. The third shelf had a variety of trophies for many different sports: bowling, golf, tennis, and swimming. The bottom shelf was full of old magazines and newspapers. In short, this bookcase was the perfect place for junk.

N   D   E

2.   Colors are traditionally classified according to a system that Albert Henry Munsell developed. The first consideration is the color's hue, or its basic color. The second is the saturation of the color. In other words, we describe a color on the basis of its intensity. The final point is the color's brightness. By using these three considerations, we can define the colors around us.

N   D   E

3.   Ellis Island is an interesting chapter in U.S. history. It was first bought by the government in 1808. At first, it was used as a fort. Later on, the army used it as an arsenal. Then, in 1891, it began the job that it became famous for. It was used as a gateway to the United States by immigration officials. Every European immigrant who came to the U.S. between 1891 and 1954 passed through Ellis Island. After 1954, it was closed. Recently, it has been reopened as a tourist attraction. Both American and foreign tourists can go there and learn about the role this small island played in the history of the United States.

N   D   E

4.   American football and rugby have both similarities and differences. Both games are played with a leather, oval-shaped ball, and both games are derived from soccer. The differences include the number of players. Football requires 11 players, whereas rugby requires 13 to 15. A football field is longer than a rugby field, but its width is less. Football has four quarters of 15 minutes each, but rugby has two 40 minute halves. A touchdown in football is worth six points. However, a goal in rugby is only worth four points. In short, football and rugby are generally the same, but the details are different.

N   D   E

5.   My train trip across the United States was a family affair. I started in Seattle, where I visited my cousin and her family. Then I went to Michigan. I met my mother's sisters and their families for the first time in my life. In New York, I saw my two brothers. The three of us had a great time seeing the sights, but we had a better time catching up on the family. All in all, this trip is one that I remember most fondly.

N   D   E

D. PREWRITING

Good writers think, plan, write a draft, think, rewrite, think, rewrite, and so on. Writing is a continuing process of thinking and organizing. The first problem lies in trying to think of what to say, and the next is organizing your material. Here are two methods for getting ideas. Sometimes you may want to do both.

Brainstorming

Brainstorming can be done individually or in groups. The purpose of brainstorming is to get together a lot of ideas without any order. The ordering comes later. If a small group is formed, one person may be made the secretary of the group. As all the members of the group come up with ideas about what they can write in the assignment, the secretary takes notes to share with the group later. It is also possible for each student to take his or her own notes. It is important to allow ALL ideas to be noted. This is not a time to evaluate how good or bad they are. After about 10 minutes, the secretary stops the discussion and reads what the group members have said. This is to remind them of all the points which have been brought up. The members of the group then go to their own seats to reflect on all the possible points to make in their own writing. Of course, an individual can go through this process alone.

Look at this example of notes from a brainstorming session on the influence of television.

TV shows — situation comedies ("Cheers")
— drama ("LA Law")
— etc

Cable — expanding industry

TV & children — cartoons
— too much violence (what about family hour?)
— ads directed at children

Good for second language learners

NEWS COVERAGE

Hollywood

Sports — Monday night football

VCR's & video recording

TV as companion

"Wheel of Fortune" — GAME SHOWS

Freewriting

Freewriting is similar to brainstorming individually on paper. You start with a word or a phrase (perhaps the topic of your assignment) and write down anything you can think of. Unlike brainstorming, you don't just list a lot of points; instead, you try to write sentences where one word leads to the next. When you get stuck, you just pick up on one of the previous words and continue writing about that. You don't worry about grammar, punctuation, or spelling because no one will see your freewriting but you. The most important aspect of freewriting is *not to allow yourself to stop.* Let your ideas and imagination flow. If you practice freewriting, you will find that some words tend to be repeated and that ideas occur to you just from writing those words.

Here is an example of freewriting. It is also about the influence of television.

> There are a lot of different shows in U.S. — comedies, dramas, movie shows on cable. there's always some show on the "tube" as my host mother calls it. Always many many shows. What does that do to people/society? What about advertising? Good points of t.v. = good for second language learners, get news and information. there's a lot of news shows - national - local. I like the national news best. It sometimes tells things about home. My neighbor - her t.v. on all the time. It's so important to her. She has a VCR and records shows.

Now that you have gotten some ideas for your paragraph, you need to organize those ideas. Here are two methods to help you do that.

Topic Outline

The next step is to organize your ideas. One way to do this is to outline the points you want to make. To write an outline, you first have to decide what the main point of the paragraph is. You usually write that point as a sentence or just as a few words on a separate line of a piece of paper. After that, you need to consider which examples, facts, steps, or arguments to include in order to show your reader that your main point is reasonable. You should pick the best ones from your brainstorming or freewriting and list them on separate lines below your main point. In an outline, you shouldn't use complete sentences. All you need are a few words which will help you remember what you are going to write. Like brainstorming and freewriting, an outline is just for you, not for anybody else. Here is a sample of a topic outline based on the previous brainstorming and freewriting.

T.V. is very important to Americans.

A. Many kinds of shows

   1. sports

   2. news

   3. Comedy

   4. drama

B. Expanding into cable

C. Video

D. TV as friend

   1. on many hours - almost always

   2. my neighbor

Circle Outline

Some people prefer another kind of outline format called a circle outline. The best thing about a circle outline is that you can easily add to it at any point. However, note that there is a system to it; the main point is in the center of the circle, and the examples are placed around that center. The sample below is a circle outline of the paragraph describing the influence of television.

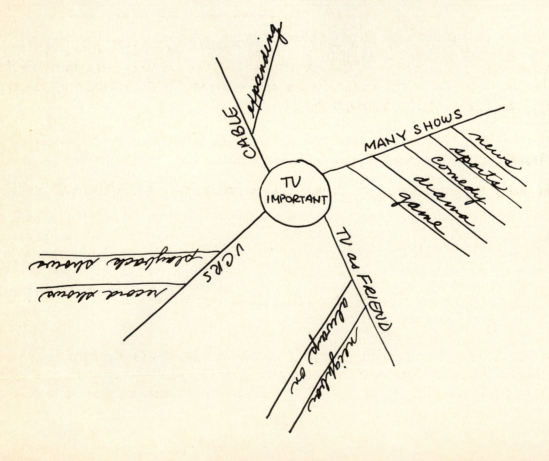

Here's the first draft of the paragraph about the influence of television on American life.

Americans really like TV. They often use it as a friend. It's always turned on when they're at home. I never have the TV turned on unless I'm watching it. There are many kinds of programs, too. There are comedies, dramas, game shows and news shows. Cable TV is becoming very popular, too. So Americans can choose from a lot of programs at any time during the day. Nowadays, VCR's are allowing Americans to use their TV's even more. I wonder if Americans could live without TV.

This is a first draft because it is not finished yet. Good writers should make sure to read their writing carefully in order to make changes and corrections in their own work before they consider it finished. The process of making these changes will be discussed in the following chapter. See page 25 for the final draft of this paragraph.

E. PARAGRAPH FORMAT

Look back at the paragraphs in this chapter. They all have a similar shape. They look like this:

```
    Xxxxxxxxxxxxxxxxxxxxxxxxxxxxxxxxx. Xxxxxxxxxx
xxxxxxxxxxxxxxxxxxxxxxxxxxxxx. Xxxxxxxxxxxxxxxxxxxxx. Xxx
xxxxxxxxxxxxxxxxxxxxxxxxxxxxxxxxxxxxxxAmericans. Xxxxxxx
xxxxxxxxxxxxx. Xxxxxxxxxxxxxxxxxxxxxxxxxxxxxxxxxxxx
xxxxxxxxxxxxxxxxxxxxx. Xxxxxxxxxxxxxxxxxxx. Xxxxxxx
xxxxxxxxxxxxxxxxxxxxxxxxxxxxxxxxx.
```

There are four things to note about this diagram. First, the first sentence starts in about six spaces. This is called indentation. All paragraphs are indented. That way, we know where one paragraph ends and another begins. The second point is that each sentence starts with a capital letter and ends with a period. The third point is that a sentence begins where the previous sentence ended. We don't go back to the beginning of the next line. The last point to consider about paragraph format is the margins. You should leave about 1" of space on either side of the paper.

Exercise 2

In groups of three to five, brainstorm one of these topics:

1. How would you recommend someone to study your native language?

2. What are the most interesting aspects of the city you live in now?

3. How would you describe this person's face?

Exercise 3

Freewrite for 10 minutes on the same topic that you discussed in your brainstorming session.

Exercise 4

Now organize your paragraph. Use either the topic or the circle outline format.

Topic Outline:

(main point) _____

_____

(examples, steps, or arguments)

_____

_____

_____

_____

Circle Outline:

F. YOU'RE IN CHARGE: WRITING TO COMMUNICATE

Write the paragraph you brainstormed and outlined, using good paragraph format. Write on every other line of your paper.

G. | PARAGRAPH CHECKLIST

If possible, it is always a good idea to set your paragraph aside for a while after you have written it. Then go back and reread it. Use the checklist below as a basis for what to look for when you reread your paragraph. Check off the items that are true for your paragraph.

> _____ 1. *I have indented my paragraph.*
>
> _____ 2. *All of my sentences begin with capital letters and end with periods.*
>
> _____ 3. *All of my sentences begin where the previous one left off.*
>
> _____ 4. *I have appropriate margins on both sides of my page.*

If one of the items above is not checked off, you need to fix your paragraph so that it can be checked off.

3 Organization of Paragraphs

Look again at this paragraph from Chapter 2. Notice that it consists of three parts in a specific pattern.

> My first full day in Yugoslavia turned out to be my worst day there. I woke up late in my small hotel room. I wanted to take a quick shower, but there was no hot water. In fact, there was only ice cold water. I went down to breakfast and was served a stale roll and lukewarm tea. Next, I got lost trying to find my way to the meeting I was already late for. I couldn't find anyone who spoke English, and my Croatian was still not very good. At last I found the meeting place, but I also found out that the meeting had been postponed to the following day. I got lost again on my way back to the hotel and spent most of the day "sightseeing" on the various city buses. Finally, I arrived back at the hotel ready for dinner. The waiter politely told me that I was too late for dinner. I went to my room tired and hungry. Little did I know that this would be my worst day, so I had nothing but good days to look forward to.

This paragraph begins with a sentence which introduces the topic of the paragraph. It's called the TOPIC SENTENCE. The middle part is called the BODY, and it consists of sentences which explain, or support, the topic sentence. These sentences are called SUPPORTING SENTENCES. The last sentence is called the CONCLUDING SENTENCE. It obviously ends the paragraph.

As you will see in Part II of this book, not all essay paragraphs in essays written by native speakers of English follow this pattern. There are, in fact, many variations in the form of essay paragraphs. Some have no topic sentence, some have the topic sentence at the end, some have no concluding sentence, and some have another kind of sentence as the last sentence in the paragraph. However, basic American writing is LINEAR in structure; that is, it has a beginning, a middle, and an end, and it proceeds directly from one part to the next. In this book, you will practice using the standard topic and concluding sentences because this is a common pattern of writing. (For samples of body paragraphs in different formats, see Chapter 10.)

A. THE TOPIC SENTENCE

A topic sentence is the most important sentence in a paragraph. It tells what the paragraph is going to be about, or its main idea. The topic sentence consists of two parts: the TOPIC and the CONTROLLING IDEA. The topic is the subject of your paragraph. It is what you are writing about. The controlling idea limits your topic to the one aspect of the topic that you want to write about.

Look at these examples.

1. New York has (excellent public transportation.)
     controlling idea
2. New York has (interesting people.)
     controlling idea

Notice that all topics have more than one possible controlling idea. You could write a paragraph about New York and its public transportation, you could write about New York and its people, or you could write about some other aspect of New York. The possibilities are endless, and each paragraph would require a different topic sentence.

All topic sentences are opinions. A simple statement of fact cannot be a topic sentence because there is nothing more to be said about it, and therefore no paragraph to write. Consider the following examples.

3. My brother is a good family man.

4. My brother is older than I am.

Sentence (4) cannot be a topic sentence. You cannot write a paragraph supporting the statement that your brother is older than you because such a statement is either true or false, and that's all. However, you could write a paragraph giving examples of how your brother is a good family man and show what you mean by that phrase. This makes sentence (3) an acceptable topic sentence.

Another type of topic sentence is the kind where you divide your topic into different parts. For example, you may write:

5. The modern study of biology consists of (three basic areas.)
     topic   *controlling idea*
6. There are (four main kinds) of love.
     controlling idea   *topic*
7. Planning a scientific experiment requires (five specific steps.)
     topic   *controlling idea*

These topic sentences look like facts, but they are not. Someone could disagree with the writer's controlling idea and say, "No, there aren't four kinds of love; there are only three." The writer needs to support his or her topic sentence by describing what those kinds of love are, and in that way persuade the reader that the sentence is reasonable.

Exercise 1

Read each sentence below. Underline the topic and circle the controlling idea in each.

1. There are many tourist attractions in San Francisco.

2. Alcohol is harmful to your health.

3. There are five stages to American education.

4. Many people eat too much junk food.

5. People who want to learn a foreign language must master four skill areas.

6. Agatha Christie is a very popular mystery writer.

7. The California condor must be saved from extinction.

8. Hollywood doesn't have any normal people.

9. There are two kinds of people in my family.

10. You need four ingredients to make peanut butter.

Exercise 2

In the chart below there are three topics followed by five possible purposes for writing a paragraph. Your job is to discuss and write down topic sentences that fit those purposes. In many cases, you will need to come up with a more specific topic. The class will be divided into groups of three to five people.

General Topic   **1. CIGARETTE SMOKING**

Purpose for Writing   to warn others

Topic Sentence   _____

_____

Purpose for Writing   to show the smoking/cancer connection

Topic Sentence   _____

_____

Purpose for Writing   to describe an advertisement

Topic Sentence   _____

_____

Purpose for Writing   to suggest techniques for quitting

Topic Sentence   _____

_____

Purpose for Writing   to argue for non-smoking restaurants

Topic Sentence   _____

_____

General Topic	**2. OUR SCHOOL**
Purpose for Writing	to describe it for a brochure
Topic Sentence	_____
	_____
Purpose for Writing	to tell its history
Topic Sentence	_____
	_____
Purpose for Writing	to compare it to another school
Topic Sentence	_____
	_____
Purpose for Writing	to narrate a typical day
Topic Sentence	_____
	_____
Purpose for Writing	to suggest improvements
Topic Sentence	_____
	_____
General Topic	**3. TELEVISION**
Purpose for Writing	to describe a program
Topic Sentence	_____
	_____
Purpose for Writing	to compare two shows
Topic Sentence	_____
	_____

Purpose for Writing   to narrate yesterday's news

Topic Sentence   _____

_____

Purpose for Writing   to evaluate a show

Topic Sentence   _____

_____

Purpose for Writing   to divide programs into types

Topic Sentence   _____

_____

B. THE BODY (SUPPORTING SENTENCES)

There are many ways to support a topic sentence. One of the most common is to use facts and/or statistics. Look at this paragraph about Colorado. Its support consists of facts and statistics.

Example 1   Colorado is an interesting state. It has 104,247 square miles and almost three million people. Since 1920, the percentage of rural dwellers has sharply decreased, going from 51.8% in 1920 to 19.4% in 1980. Colorado is called the Centennial State because it joined the Union in 1876, one hundred years after the U.S. declared its independence. Colorado's main industries today are mining, manufacturing, agriculture, and tourism. As most residents would say, Colorado is a great state.

We could also write a paragraph about Colorado and support it with specific examples. Look at this paragraph.

Example 2   Colorado is an interesting state. It is perhaps best known as the Rocky Mountain State. Indeed, these mountains seem to dominate most views in Colorado. Denver and Colorado Springs are the state's two largest cities. Both have unique identities. Not far outside Denver is Red Rocks. This is a beautiful natural amphitheater where some of Denver's most memorable concerts have been staged. In the southwest corner of the state is Mesa Verde, where there are ancient Indian cliff dwellings. All in all, Colorado is a great state.

The third way of supporting a topic sentence is with the use of illustration. This is usually based on personal experience. Here is a final paragraph on Colorado. Notice that the support is based on a personal experience.

Example 3   Colorado is an interesting state. On our vacation there last summer, we went hiking in the Rocky Mountains. These mountains stretch from north to south through the entire state. We also visited my cousin who lives in Denver. The U.S. Mint was the most fascinating place in that city for me. Later on, we saw some old Indian dwellings in Mesa Verde. These houses were actually built in cliffs! Colorado is definitely a great state for a vacation.

Of course, you, as the writer, must decide which of these three different ways of supporting a paragraph is the best for the particular paragraph that you want to write.

C. THE CONCLUDING SENTENCE

The concluding sentence of a paragraph is generally of one of two types. The first type is a restatement of the topic sentence. You simply say the same thing again, but you use different words. Notice the concluding sentence in this paragraph. It is a restatement of the topic sentence.

Example 1   Alcohol is harmful to your health. It primarily damages the liver. A long period of alcohol abuse can cause cirrhosis of the liver, and it has recently been determined that even cancer of the liver can be caused by too much alcohol. Of course, the entire gastrointestinal system can be damaged as well. Too much alcohol may also cause insomnia, amnesia, and loss of control of the body. In fact, it may permanently damage the nervous system. In many ways, alcohol is not good for your body.

The second way of concluding a paragraph is by summarizing the main points that were made in the paragraph. Here is an example of a paragraph with a concluding sentence that is a summary.

Example 2   There are five stages to American education. The first stage is nursery school or pre-school. This is for children from ages three to five. Once a child reaches age five, he/she goes to elementary school, which is also called primary school. Usually, children go to elementary school for six years. Then, at age 11-12, children go to junior high school. Junior high school lasts for two years in some places but three years in other schools. After junior high school comes high school. Students begin this school at ages 14 or 15, depending on how long they went to junior high school. Students remain in high school for three or four years, again depending on how long their junior high school experience was. After graduation from high school, students have the option of going on to college, where they could remain for any number of years. In short, children in the U.S. may go through nursery school, elementary school, junior high school, high school, and college.

Note that this concluding sentence lists the major points that were discussed in this paragraph. This is a "summary" concluding sentence.

D. YOU'RE IN CHARGE: WRITING TO COMMUNICATE

Pick one of the topics, purposes, and controlling ideas that you discussed in Exercise 2 (pages 21–23). Start your thinking by silent brainstorming or freewriting. Next, write a simple outline in any format you choose. Finally, write your paragraph on every other line of the paper.

E. REWRITING

Because rewriting is an important part of the writing process, all good writers rewrite. Rewriting actually consists of two processes: revising and editing.

Revising is the first step. You may start revising as soon as you finish writing, or it is often even better to set your paragraph aside for a while and get back to it later. Read what you have written, and ask yourself these questions: "Have I said what I wanted to say?" and "Have I made myself clear to the reader?" These are questions about the content of the piece of writing. During the revising part of rewriting, you also need to ask yourself about the organization of your paragraph. "Does this paragraph have a topic sentence?" and "What is my topic and controlling idea?" are the basic questions to ask.

Below is the paragraph from Chapter 2 which was the result of prewriting. Read the original paragraph and look at the notes the writer has made to him/herself. Then read the revised paragraph. The writer has made some changes. Are there any other changes you would like to make?

> *more specific*   *over generalization*
>
> Americans (really like TV.) They often use it as a friend. It's (always) turned
> on when they're at home. ~~I never have the TV on unless I'm watching it.~~ There   *not necessary*
> are many kinds of programs, too. There are comedies, dramas, game shows,— *give examples*
> and news shows. Cable TV is becoming very popular, too. (So) Americans can   *vocab.*
> *examples* — choose from a lot of programs at any time during the day. Nowadays, VCR's
> are allowing Americans to use their TV's even more. I wonder if Americans
> could live without TV.   *How?*

Now read the rewrite of the paragraph after it has been revised.

> Television is an integral part of American life. Many Americans have the
> TV turned on whenever they're at home. It seems to be a companion for them.
> Also, there are many programs for people to choose from. There are comedies
> such as *Cheers*, dramas such as *L.A. Law*, game shows such as *Wheel of For-
> tune*, and an abundance of both local and national news shows. Cable TV
> expands the number of shows available to watch at any given time of the day.
> In addition, most Americans have VCRs which allow them to use their TVs
> even more and never to miss a show even when they're not at home! In short,
> I doubt that most Americans could live without TV.

The writer here felt he or she needed a topic sentence. The writer also wanted to be more specific about how he or she felt and to give concrete examples of TV shows and the uses of TV.

The other aspect of rewriting is editing. This is basically checking spelling, punctuation, vocabulary, and grammar. Editing is usually rather mechanical. The rules of spelling, for example, are clear; a word is either right or wrong. In grammar and punctuation as well, there are many cases where we can say that something is wrong and something else is right. Your classmates and your teacher can help you write better and more correctly by using editing symbols as feedback on your writing. You can find a list of some of these symbols in Appendix 4, page 153.

Finally, there are also times when you and your teacher will feel that one sentence is better than another even though there is nothing really wrong with the original sentence. This is the area where revising and editing meet. Becoming a better writer is a process of combining these two aspects of rewriting in order to truly communicate what you want the reader to understand.

F. PEER EDITING

Give the paragraph that you wrote in Section D of this chapter to another student in your class. Read that student's paragraph while he or she reads yours. Write question marks in the margin for sentences or words you don't understand and try to use some correction symbols. Make notes at the bottom of the page about changing the topic sentence, adding or deleting (taking away) examples, or any other aspects that you think would make your classmate's paragraph better. Then give the paragraphs back to each other and discuss the possible changes. Finally, rewrite your own paragraph, editing it the way you think it should be.

G. | PARAGRAPH CHECKLIST |

Here is another paragraph checklist. Use it when you reread your paragraph. Remember, if you can't check off an item, you need to go back to your paragraph and change it.

_____ 1. *I have a topic sentence which has the main idea of my paragraph.*

_____ 2. *I have underlined the topic and circled the controlling idea.*

3. *The body of my paragraph consists of* (Check one.)

_____ *facts and statistics.*

_____ *specific examples.*

_____ *personal experience.*

4. *My concluding sentence* (Check one.)

_____ *restates the topic sentence.*

_____ *summarizes the topic sentence.*

---

4 Coherence and Cohesion

A. CHRONOLOGICAL ORDERING

Read the following paragraph.

> We had a wonderful time at the Bruce Springsteen concert last night. At first, Bruce came on stage and started singing "Born in the U.S.A." Next, the people in the audience started dancing to the song, too. After that, he told a funny story. The people in the audience roared with laughter. Later on, Bruce told another story. This time, the story was sad, and the people in the audience cried. Finally, when Bruce left the stage after four hours, the audience screamed for more. Then, he started dancing to this song. It was truly a memorable evening.

What does the topic sentence (the first sentence) tell you about this paragraph? What kind of paragraph is it?

You can guess that this is a narrative paragraph because of the topic sentence. The supporting sentences, too, tell about events, but the order of events is somewhat mixed up. This can make the paragraph difficult to understand. For a narrative paragraph you must use good CHRONO-LOGICAL ORDERING of sentences if you want a clear paragraph. This means that the supporting sentences must tell the story's events in the order that they happened. In other words, the events must be ordered according to TIME.

This principle of good ordering of supporting sentences is one of the characteristics that a good paragraph must have. When a narrative paragraph uses good chronological ordering, then the COHERENCE of the paragraph is good. Coherence is the good ordering of sentences in a paragraph.

Now look back at the beginning paragraph. This paragraph does not have good coherence. There is one sentence which is out of order. Can you find that sentence? Place it where it should be so that the paragraph will have good coherence.

Exercise 1

Here is another narrative paragraph which does not have good coherence. Can you fix it?

> The rainy day last Saturday caused me to be very lazy. At five o'clock, I noticed that it was getting dark but that the rain hadn't stopped. When I woke up and heard the rain, I decided that it would be much better to stay in bed a little longer. After a while, I got out of bed and made some tea. Next, I wrapped myself in a blanket and sat in my favorite chair reading a book. Later on in the afternoon, I noticed that my favorite movie was on television. While I watched it, I cried as I usually do. I had been lazy all day, but I didn't care.

B. SPATIAL ORDERING

Descriptive paragraphs also need good coherence, or good ordering of sentences. However, they do not use chronological ordering. They use SPATIAL ORDERING. In other words, they have sentences that are ordered according to SPACE. Usually, this means that items are described systematically through space. For example, this could be top to bottom, head to foot, left to right, or front to back. Look at this paragraph. It does not have good spatial ordering.

My cat is a typically mischievious feline. At the end of her body is a long tail which is constantly in motion. Her fur is white, and this makes the perky ears on top of her head look a little pink. Her eyes are big and yellow. When she's wide awake and in trouble, they can look as bright as the sun. Her nose is pink, and under this is her mouth. It is usually open and talking, or it has a sly smile on it. On both sides of her mouth are whiskers. These are long and seem to dance in the sunlight. This seemingly innocent head is attached to a rather plump, but hardly lazy, body. Her legs are strong and allow her to make an escape in a matter of minutes. In short, I have to say that I love this little trouble-maker of mine.

Find the sentence that is out of order in this paragraph. Where would you put it so that this paragraph will have good coherence?

Exercise 2

Read the following descriptive paragraph. It does not have good spatial ordering. Find the sentence which is out of order and put it in the correct place. If you can't tell, try drawing a floorplan of this room. This may help you decide which sentence is out of order.

The Language Lab looked very ordered. As I entered, I saw several rows of booths to the left. At the front of the rows was a console where the teacher sat facing class. Each booth had a tape player and headphones. To the right of the console was a big T.V. screen with video-playing capacity. On the wall opposite the rows of booths, there were three plain doors. I knew that this was a place where I had to work hard.

C. EXPLANATORY ORDERING

As you might guess by now, expository paragraphs also require good coherence. The principle, however, is different. The principle is not time as it is with narrative paragraphs, nor is it space as it is with descriptive paragraphs. With expository paragraphs, coherence depends on a clear system of explanation. Expository paragraphs have sentences ordered by EXPLANATORY ORDERING. Look at this example of an expository paragraph which does *not* have good coherence.

Ten-speed bicycles and tricycles are both people-powered means of transportation, but there are obvious differences. The first difference is in the number of wheels. Of course, this difference in the number of wheels is due to the difference in the kind of rider. A ten-speed bicycle has two wheels, whereas a tricycle has three wheels. A ten-speed is ridden by someone who is able to balance a bicycle on two wheels. On the other hand, a tricycle is ridden by someone who doesn't have this skill. The final obvious difference between a ten-speed and a tricycle is that a ten-speed has ten gears. It is designed to do many kinds of riding, but a tricycle has only one speed and offers one kind of riding. In conclusion, ten-speeds and tricycles have differences that are easy to see at a glance.

Which of these sentences is out of order? Find it, and then put it in its proper place in the paragraph.

Exercise 3

Once again, you must make this expository paragraph have good coherence by finding the sentence which is out of order and putting it in its proper position in the paragraph.

The modern orchestra is divided into four distinct groups. The first group is the strings. Their sound is produced by vibrating strings or wires. Woodwind instruments make up the second section of an orchestra. These instruments, such as flutes, piccolos and oboes, make their sound by the player blowing into a mouthpiece and opening and closing holes in the instrument. The third section is the brass section, whose instruments make sounds by the vibration of the player's lips on a mouthpiece. Examples of brass instruments are bugles, trumpets and tubas. Examples of string instruments are violins, cellos and basses. The last section of an orchestra is the percussion section. The sound of these instruments is made by hitting them. Examples of percussion instruments include cymbals, drums and tambourines. When put together, these four groups of instruments make a complete orchestra.

D. COHESIVE DEVICES

Another characteristic that a paragraph must have is COHESION. When a paragraph has cohesion, all of the supporting sentences "stick together" and are related in their support of the topic sentence. In other words, they are connected to each other.

Linking Words

There are many ways to help a paragraph have cohesion. One way is to use LINKING WORDS. The most common type of linking word is TRANSITIONS. Transitions are words that help to relate sentences to one another. (They may also help the coherence of a paragraph by indicating the order of the supporting sentences.) To some extent, linking words, including transitions, are particular to the type of paragraph that you are writing. Narrative paragraphs, for example, usually use the following transitions.

first, second, third, etc.
at first
next
after that
later on
then
finally

Look back at the narrative paragraphs in this chapter in which you have reordered the sentences. Underline all of the linking words (in this case transitions) that these paragraphs have. Notice how these words connect the sentences in the paragraphs.

As you might expect, there are linking words for descriptive and expository paragraphs as well. The linking words of descriptive paragraphs are usually prepositions of place. Here are some examples of prepositions of place that can be used to connect the sentences in a descriptive paragraph.

to the left
to the right
on both sides
in front of
behind
on top of
under
on/at the end
above
next to

The linking words for expository paragraphs are transitions. In fact, some are the same as those that can be used for narrative paragraphs as this list shows.

first, second, third, etc.
however
on the other hand
in fact
therefore
furthermore
finally
in conclusion

Once again, go back to the descriptive and expository paragraphs you have worked with in this chapter. Underline the linking words and notice how they help the supporting sentences "stick together." This is good cohesion. (For a summary of linking words used in this text, see Appendix 2.)

Pronouns

In addition to linking words, there are other ways to help a paragraph have good cohesion. One of them is by using PRONOUNS. Pronouns almost always have antecedents, or nouns that they stand for, in previous sentences. In other words, a pronoun in one sentence means that it is related to a previous sentence—the sentence which has its antecedent in it. For example, look at these two sentences.

1. The little boy looked at the ice cream cone longingly.

2. He grabbed it and ate it.

Using pronouns in the second sentence connects these two sentences. In fact, if you didn't use pronouns in the second sentence, you would have an awkward sentence which may or may not be related to the first sentence. This is shown in the examples below.

1. The little boy looked at the ice cream cone longingly.

2. The little boy grabbed the ice cream cone and ate the ice cream cone.

The Definite Article

A third way to connect sentences is to use the definite article (the). The definite article is almost always used after an antecedent. Therefore, a sentence with a definite article usually relates to a previous sentence. Look at these two sentences.

1. I bought an album yesterday.

2. The album is great for dancing.

It's obvious that these two sentences are talking about the same album because of the use of the definite article in the second sentence. Indeed, if the article were not used, these two sentences would not be related. Look at these two sentences.

1. I bought an album yesterday.

2. An album is great for dancing.

Demonstrative Pronouns

Another way to connect sentences in a paragraph, or to give the paragraph good cohesion, is to use demonstrative pronouns (this, that, these, those). Demonstrative pronouns, like previous cohesive devices, require antecedents, so they help connect sentences to ones that came before. Look at these two sentences.

1. On top of the table was a lamp.

2. This lamp had a crooked shade.

Of course, you could use a definite article instead of the demonstrative pronoun to indicate that the two sentences go together. However, you must use one or the other. If you don't, then these two sentences aren't connected.

1. On top of the table was a lamp.

2. A lamp had a crooked shade.

Synonyms

The use of synonyms can also be considered a cohesive device. Like using a pronoun, using a synonym prevents the frequent repetition of a word or words while connecting two sentences. For example, the following paragraph is awkward because of the overrepetition of words.

Example 1   The frustrated waiter shouted at everyone. He shouted at the customers to take their seats quickly. He became frustrated because they didn't order quickly enough, so he shouted at them to order. Then, he shouted the order to the cook. After several frustrating hours of this, the boss finally shouted at the waiter, "You're fired!"

Now read a similar paragraph which uses synonyms.

Example 2   The upset waiter shouted at everyone. He yelled at the customers to take their seats quickly. He became angry because they didn't order fast enough, so he spoke to them sternly about ordering. Then he screamed the order to the cook. After several trying hours of this, the boss finally shouted to the waiter, "You're fired!"

To sum up, cohesive devices, such as linking words, pronouns, definte articles, demonstrative pronouns and synonyms, are useful in relating sentences in a paragraph to one another. When sentences are related, your paragraph has good cohesion.

Exercise 4

The paragraph below lacks cohesion because it doesn't have linking words, definite articles and demonstrative pronouns and because it repeats nouns instead of using pronouns or synonyms. Rewrite the paragraph in the space provided. Make the cohesion better by adding appropriate linking words, by using definite articles or demonstrative pronouns where the indefinte pronoun is wrong, and by substituting a pronoun or a synonym for noun phrases that have been repeated too many times.

Traveling to a foreign city can be fun, but traveling to a foreign city requires some planning besides getting a passport. You should buy a phrase book and learn a few key phrases in a foreign language. Using phrases demonstrates a willingness to learn about the people who live in a foreign city. Read about a city beforehand. Read about what places in a foreign city you'd like to see.

Get a feeling for a foreign city and for weather so that you can pack appropriate clothes. Check your camera. Make sure that your camera is in good working order and that you have lots of film. Get yourself a good pair of walking shoes, and break a good pair of walking shoes in for about a month before you leave. Taking a few precautions before you leave can make your trip to a foreign city more enjoyable.

_____

_____

_____

_____

_____

_____

_____

_____

_____

_____

_____

_____

_____

_____

Exercise 5

Below are three paragraphs, each of which has some problems with coherence and cohesion. Read each paragraph and then make the changes necessary to make it a better paragraph. Follow this procedure.

a. Identify any sentences which may be out of order. (Only two of the paragraphs have sentences out of order.) Put the sentence in the correct position.

b. Fill in each blank with an appropriate linking word. You may want to identify the type of paragraph each is to help you do this. Look back at the list of linking words on page 30.

c. Follow the specific instructions at the beginning of each paragraph.

1. CHANGE ONE NOUN INTO ITS PRONOUN.

The California Gold Rush changed California almost over night. The population went from 15,000 to 300,000. One day in 1848, a miner discovered gold in the American River. _____ _____, news of the discovery spread quickly. In 1849, literally thousands of people came to California. Thousands of people all wanted to find gold and become rich. Finally, in 1850, California had enough people to become a state in the Union. All of these changes happened in just two years due to the discovery of gold.

2. CHANGE AN INDEFINITE ARTICLE INTO A DEFINITE ARTICLE.

The lamp on my desk looks functional but not pretty. The base of the lamp is a 8″ × 4″ × 2″ block which appears to be made of wood but which is actually made of plastic. A 1″ × 1″ × 6″ piece of plastic wood rises from the middle of the back end of the base. _____ this piece is a metal, snakelike bar which is about 6″ in length. At the end of this is the lamp itself, which is parallel to the base of the lamp. The bulb of a lamp is a fluorescent one; it is about 15″ in length. This lamp obviously belongs in an office and not in a living room. This bulb is partially covered by a white plastic lamp shade.

3. CHANGE A PHRASE INTO A DEMONSTRATIVE PRONOUN.

After students graduate from high school in the U.S., they have three choices of what to do. The first choice is to go to a four-year university. To go to a four-year university is not always possible because students need good grades and lots of money. Students who have less money or not so good grades can choose a two-year community college. This can be a wise decision because community colleges offer vocational classes and university preparation classes. _____, the third choice is to get a job. However, it is hard to get a good job with only a high school education. All U.S. students have this important decision to make upon graduation.

E. YOU'RE IN CHARGE: WRITING TO COMMUNICATE

1. Write a paragraph about one of the topics below. Be sure to use linking words, pronouns, definite articles, demonstrative pronouns and synonyms where appropriate. Instead of using good paragraph format this time, write each of the sentences in your paragraph on a separate line. After you are finished, cut your paragraph into strips so that each strip has one sentence on it. Mix your sentences up and exchange them with a classmate's. Reorder the sentences of your classmate's paragraph while he/she reorders yours.

   Topics: an enjoyable evening (NARRATIVE)
   my best friend (DESCRIPTIVE)
   options for a high school graduate in my country (EXPOSITORY)

2. Here is a floor plan of a typical college dormitory room. Write a descriptive paragraph about this room. Remember that you should use good spatial ordering. Also, you should try to make the controlling idea in your topic sentence an impression that you have of this room. Use good paragraph format.

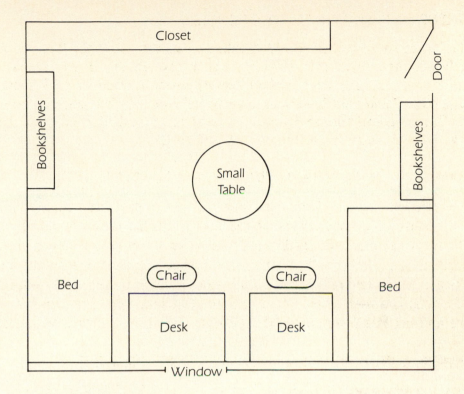

F. PARAGRAPH CHECKLIST

Use this Paragraph Checklist to check your paragraph for good coherence and your use of cohesive devises. Look back in the chapter for an explanation of any terms you don't recall.

_____ 1. *I have a topic sentence.*

_____ 2. *I have underlined the topic and circled the controlling idea.*

_____ 3. *My paragraph has good coherence.*
It follows (Check one.)

    _____ *chronological order.*

    _____ *spatial order.*

    _____ *explanatory order.*

4. *I have used the following as cohesive devices.*
(Check as many as appropriate.)

_____ *linking words*

_____ *pronouns*

_____ *definite articles*

_____ *demonstrative pronouns*

_____ *synonyms*

5 Unity and Completeness

A. UNITY

As you have seen, a good paragraph in English must have three separate parts (a topic sentence, supporting sentences, and a concluding sentence) as well as certain characteristics. In Chapter 4, you read about coherence and cohesion. Another paragraph characteristic is UNITY. If a paragraph has this characteristic, then all of the supporting sentences relate to the topic sentence. Look at the following paragraph. Read each of the supporting sentences carefully. Does each relate to the topic sentence?

> The Smithsonian Institute, located in Washington, D.C., has a dual purpose for the people of the United States. The first purpose is to do fundamental research. It then publishes the findings of this research. The second, and perhaps best-known, purpose is to maintain a group of museums. These museums are designed to preserve the history and culture of the U.S. Some of the most famous of these museums are the National Air and Space Museum, the National Gallery of Art and the National Museum of Natural History. The President of the United States also lives in Washington, D.C. These two functions of the Smithsonian Institute are very important to the American people.

Since this is a paragraph about the Smithsonian Institute, all of the sentences should talk about that. However, the sentence about the President of the United States is not about the Smithsonian Institute. Therefore, it does not belong in this paragraph and should be crossed out. When a sentence does not belong in a paragraph, it is called an IRRELEVANT SENTENCE.

Exercise 1

Find the irrelevant sentences in the following paragraphs. Cross them out so that the paragraph will have good paragraph unity.

1.   My great aunt has a face full of character. The hair on top of her head is silver gray and falls gently over her wrinkled forehead. Her eyebrows are also gray. Under these are her marvelous eyes. They are blue and shine as brightly as they did on the day she was born. My great aunt lives in a town *— irrelevant* in Missouri, so I don't get to visit her often. Her cheeks are wrinkled, but they are also rosy. Her nose is a bit crooked due to a childhood break. Under her nose is her mouth, which always seems to have a sweet smile on it. Her chin is also wrinkled and has a prominent scar in the middle. All in all, her face is one which has always brought me great comfort.

2.   The Suez Canal and the Panama Canal have similar histories. Today many *irrel* tourists visit both canals. The same Frenchman, de Lesseps, controlled the initial building of both canals. The Suez Canal was begun in 1859 by the Suez Canal Company. This company was controlled by the French. Likewise, the French bought a Colombian canal-building company in 1881 in order to build the Panama Canal. Americans finally finished that canal. In the end, however, both canals finally came under control of the countries in which they are located. Egypt gained control of the Suez Canal in 1957 by fighting France and Britain. Panama gained control over its canal peaceably in 1977. These similarities took place about 20 years apart and provided the world with two important waterways.

Exercise 2

This exercise is similar to the previous exercise, but it is a little bit more difficult. You are still looking for irrelevant sentences, but there may be more than one in each paragraph or there may be no irrelevant sentences. Cross out all the irrelevant sentences that you find.

1.   Valentine's Day can be a miserable day if you don't have a girl/boyfriend. You see red hearts and cupids everywhere. You also seem to see more pictures of people in love, not to mention more actual people on the streets who are obviously in love. Of course, you walk on the streets alone. I much prefer Thanksgiving because it is more of a family holiday. I have lots of family members who love me. *irrel* Commercials on TV tell you about all the wonderful presents and cards that you can buy for that "special someone" for Valentine's Day. You watch the commercials knowing very well that you don't have a "special someone" and that you are not a "special someone" for someone else. In addition, all of this starts happening up to three or four weeks before the actual holiday on February 14th. In my experience, it is best to leave the country if you are alone on Valentine's Day.

2.   The hotel room was small and unwelcoming. When I opened the door, a musty smell hit me. On the left side of the door, there was a beat-up, old night stand with a lamp on it. Next to the night stand was a bed with a worn bedspread on it. Above the bed, someone had hung a very ugly picture of two racehorses. A window that looked onto a parking lot was against the bed on the other side. The wall opposite the painting was blank, and there was a small desk against it. To the left of the desk was the door to the bathroom. An uglier room seemed hard to imagine.

order of ideas

3.   The children enjoyed the wonderful rides at Disneyland. They rode the train around the park, the Skyride above the park and the submarine ride under the water. They also rode on all of the rollercoasters: Space Mountain, the Matterhorn, and Thunder Mountain. They ate a delicious lunch at the Bear Cafe. Later on, on Main Street, they rode in old cars and horse-drawn carriages. Then, in Fantasyland, they rode on Mr. Toad's Wild Ride, Peter Pan's Ride, the Spinning Teacups and the Carousel. Just before leaving, they stopped in the Emporium, where they all bought a souvenir of their day at Disneyland. In short, the rides were the best part of the children's trip to Disneyland.

B. COMPLETENESS

There is one more paragraph characteristic which is necessary if a paragraph is to be well written. This is called COMPLETENESS. Completeness is like unity, but, instead of having too many sentences (some being irrelevant), there aren't enough sentences to follow through on what a topic sentence promises. As an example, look at this paragraph. Pay particular attention to the topic sentence.

> Jack had three more things to do at the library before he could go home. First, he had to find a recent article about the Stock Market. This was the topic that he had chosen to do a report about for his economics class. Second, he had to type his English essay because it was due the following day. Jack doesn't have a typewriter at home, so he always uses the library's typewriters. At last, Jack could go home.

This is an example of a paragraph which is not complete. The topic sentence says that Jack had to do three things at the library, but the paragraph only talks about two of these things. A third task must be added to this paragraph for it to be complete.

Sometimes, whether a paragraph is complete or not isn't quite so obvious. Look at this paragraph. It also isn't complete, but the reason isn't as apparent as it was in the last example.

> Doing laundry isn't much fun, but it isn't difficult either. First, gather all the dirty clothes and separate them into three piles: whites, coloreds and permanent press. Next, put the clothes into three separate washing machines. Make sure that the appropriate dials are set for the three kinds of laundry. Then, add the laundry detergent. You may want to add a softening sheet to the dryer. Finally, take the clothes out of the dryer and fold them. Although laundry isn't the most exciting activity, it is nice to have clean clothes.

This paragraph is somewhat confusing because the clothes aren't transfered from the washer to the dryer. This is a relatively important step that has been left out. For this paragraph to be complete, you would have to add a sentence which would indicate this step.

Exercise 3

Read each paragraph below. Decide if it is complete or not. If one isn't complete, be prepared to say why.

1.   The working mother must try to deal with the three separate parts of her life. First, she is a mother with certain responsibilities to the child (or children) she has brought into the world. This is not to say that her husband can't help her with these duties, but she must do her share. Second, she is a professional who has tasks to perform at work. Depending on the position that she holds, she may be responsible for managing people or money. With all of these things going on in her life, the working mother must have super-woman capabilities.

2.   If you are planning to visit San Francisco, there are several places that you shouldn't miss. Probably the most famous sight is the Golden Gate Bridge. It was built in 1937 and is still as striking today as it was then. Golden Gate Park is also a lovely place to visit on a nice day. The De Young Museum as well as a Japanese Tea Garden is located there. You must visit Fisherman's Wharf, where you can get a delicious meal of your favorite seafood. Chinatown on Grant Street is famous for its good food, too. In addition, if you want good chocolate, Ghiradelli Square is the place to go. These attractions and many more have made San Francisco the popular tourist place that it is.

3.   With Halloween just around the corner, it's important to know how to carve a pumpkin. The first step is to gather these materials together: a large pumpkin, a sharp carving knife, a big spoon, a black marking pen, a candle and some newspaper. Spread the newspaper on a table and place the pumpkin on top of it. Then, use the spoon to take out the seeds from the inside of the pumpkin. Next, with the marking pen, draw eyes, a nose and a mouth on one side of the pumpkin. These should be made in shapes that can be cut out. The next step is to do just that: carefully cut out the eyes, nose and mouth with the knife. Put a lighted candle inside of the pumpkin, and put the top back on the pumpkin. Finally, put it in a window after dark on Halloween night. It is sure to amuse your trick-or-treaters.

C. YOU'RE IN CHARGE: WRITING TO COMMUNICATE

1. Your assignment is to write a descriptive paragraph. Follow these instructions.

Instead of brainstorming in the usual way, try a different approach with your classmates. Three volunteers are needed for this. Each student (including volunteers) will need a piece of paper divided into three parts. One at a time, each volunteer should sit in a chair in front of the class. He/she should try very hard to make a certain impression for the rest of the group by sitting in the chair. In other words, each volunteer should try to show an emotion by the way he or she is sitting in the chair. The other students should sketch each of the volunteers in one of the parts on their papers. Here is an example of a sketch of a woman sitting in a chair. Your sketches should be like this.

Under each sketch, students should write down adjectives that describe the impression that the student in the chair is giving. (A note to volunteers: Make sure that you make a different impression from the ones made by previous volunteers. Also, you should sketch the other two volunteers.)

After the sketches are complete, the planning and the writing begin. Pick one of the sketches that you have drawn. Your descriptive paragraph should be about this person. Here is a paragraph written about the sketch on page 40. Notice how the impression in the controlling idea is supported throughout the paragraph.

> Miss Jones appears to be a very proper person. Her hair and make-up are very neat. She has a calm expression on her face. Her head is held high, and her back is straight against the back of this simple wooden chair. Her hands are folded on her lap. Her knees are together, and her legs are parallel to the front legs of the chair. Her feet are also together, and they rest, without movement, on the floor. When you look at Miss Jones sitting in the chair, you have to wonder if she ever relaxes.

As you plan, remember that the topic in your topic sentence is the person that you are going to describe. The controlling idea can be one of the adjectives that you wrote under the sketch. Your plan should be to describe the person from the top of the head to the feet. Remember to try to support the impression in your controlling idea throughout the paragraph. Use good paragraph format.

2. Look at the pictures here and on the next page. Each one suggests a story. Pick your favorite one and write a narrative paragraph. Remember that your paragraph should have three parts: a topic sentence with a clear topic and a clear controlling idea, supporting sentences, and a concluding sentence. Use good paragraph format.

②

③ ④

D. PARAGRAPH CHECKLIST

If possible, it is always a good idea to set your paragraph aside for a while after you have written it. Then go back and reread it. Use the checklist below as a basis for what to look for when you reread your paragraph. Check off the items that are true for your paragraph.

_____ 1. *I have a topic sentence at the beginning of my paragraph. Underline the topic and circle the controlling idea.*

_____ 2. *My paragraph does not have any irrelevant sentences. It has unity.*

_____ 3. *My paragraph is complete. There are no missing parts.*

_____ 4. *My paragraph follows*   (Circle one.)

    a. spatial ordering

    b. chronological ordering

    c. explanatory ordering

_____ 5. *I have used good paragraph format, including indentation and margins.*

If one of the items above is not checked off, you need to fix your paragraph so that it can be checked off.

PART II

The Essay

6 From Paragraph to Essay

A. EXPANDING THE PARAGRAPH

As you know, a paragraph consists of three parts: a topic sentence, supporting sentences (body), and a concluding sentence. Similarly, an essay is composed of three sections: an introductory paragraph, supporting paragraphs, and a concluding paragraph.

Some paragraphs can be expanded quite simply to essay length. Look at the paragraph from Chapter 2 about personal computers which is reprinted below. Put boxes around the three parts of this paragraph. (See page 19 for a paragraph with similar boxing.)

Example 1   Personal Computers

> A personal computer consists of three main components which have different functions. The first is the central processing unit, or CPU. This is the brain of the computer. This unit contains the memory of the machine and the microchips which make the computer able to perform its functions. The CPU has one or more disk drives, where we can put program diskettes to make the machine add numbers, do word-processing, or play games. The second component is the monitor. This looks much like a small TV, but of course it doesn't have any channel buttons. On the monitor screen we can observe what we are telling the computer to do, such as move words, draw figures, or shoot down space aliens. The third component is the keyboard. It has the shape of a typewriter keyboard with letters and numbers, but, in addition, it also contains specialized keys for computing: function keys, cursor movement arrows, and command keys. We use the keyboard to write and edit the text we want. With a CPU, a monitor, and a keyboard, we have a complete computer.

Now look at the following diagram to see how a paragraph such as this can be expanded into an essay. The topic sentence of the paragraph becomes the THESIS STATEMENT of the essay at the *end* of the introductory paragraph. The paragraph body with its description of the three parts of a computer is divided into three separate supporting paragraphs in the essay. Finally, the concluding sentence is expanded and made into a concluding paragraph.

Two other aspects of the diagram are important to note. First, see how each body paragraph mirrors the construction of the original paragraph. Just as the paragraphs you have written so far have a topic sentence, supporting sentences, and a concluding sentence, so does each body paragraph. Second, notice how the body paragraphs support the essay thesis statement as the supporting sentences in a paragraph support the topic sentence.

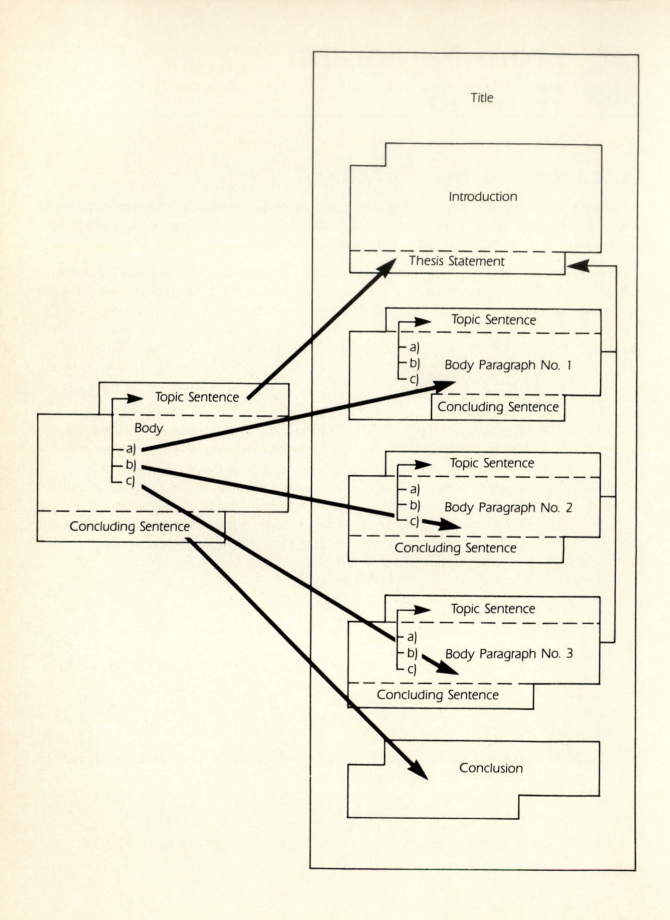

The following essay is an expansion of the paragraph about personal computers. First, draw boxes around the three components of the essay (introductory paragraph, supporting paragraphs, and concluding paragraph). Next, using another color pen, underline the topic and concluding sentences in each body paragraph.

Example 2   Personal Computers

Of all modern technological inventions, the computer is probably the most useful. There are many kinds of computers, from large mainframes to small lap-top machines, but most people are best acquainted with the personal computer. A personal computer consists of three main components which have different functions.

The first component is the central processing unit, or CPU. This is the brain of the computer. It contains the memory of the machine and the microchips which make the computer able to perform its functions. By memory we mean storage capacity, that is, the amount of space the machine has internally to store information. Most CPUs also have one or more disk drives, where we can put program diskettes to make the machine add numbers, do word-processing (writing), or play games. The CPU is, in fact, that part of the computer which "computes."

The second component is the monitor. This looks very much like a TV, but of course it doesn't have any channel buttons. Monitors come in basically two kinds: black and white and color. The monitor has a screen just like a TV, and on this screen we can observe what we are telling the computer to do, such as move words around, draw figures and charts, or play video games. Although the monitor isn't necessary to make the computer work, it sure helps to see what you are doing. The monitor is, for me, an essential component of the computer.

The third component is the keyboard. It has the shape of a typewriter keyboard with letters and numbers, but, in addition, it also contains specialized keys for computing: function keys, cursor movement arrows, and command keys. The function keys usually have numbers such as F1, F2, etc. Combined with the command keys, they can create as many as 40 different functions. Some of these functions are underlining the text, setting the margins, or listing the files you have on a disk. The cursor movement arrows move the little blinking light up or down, right or left. With these you can edit your work at any point. Command keys are keys with special built-in functions such as setting capital letters, printing, adding, or deleting. We use this keyboard to create and change the text we want.

With a CPU, a monitor, and a keyboard, we have a complete computer. Once you are familiar with these three components, you can learn to use any personal computer. Perhaps you should type your next essay on a computer?

VOCABULARY
laptop = a computer you can have on your lap
microchips = the small, central parts of the computer
keyboard = the part of a typewriter or a computer which has the letters and
    numbers that you push
keys (on a computer/typewriter) = buttons you push
function keys = keys which have special uses
command keys = keys which are used in combination with the functions keys
cursor = the flashing light which tells you where you are in a text

Here is another expository paragraph which can also be expanded into an essay by following the diagram on page 48. The topic concerns a foreign student's experiences in the United States.

Example 3   Small Things

    Three of my experiences in this country stand out in my memory as typically American. First of all, I remember coming down to breakfast at my host family's house on my first day there. My host mother had already left for work, her two children were pouring some cereal into bowls, and their father was talking on the phone. He waved to me, smiled, and pointed to the refrigerator. I didn't understand, so I just smiled. I went to school hungry that day. The second experience was trying to take a shower. I had no idea what the different knobs were for and struggled for about half an hour. Finally I gave up and had a cold bath. The third incident occurred later that week when I went to the supermarket to get some groceries. In my country we always bag our own purchases, so after I had put my food up on the counter, I went to the other end of the register, pulled out a bag, and started loading up my groceries. Someone came running up and grabbed my bag. I thought she was stealing my food and held on tight. When I finally found out what was going on, I was so embarrassed that I didn't think I could ever go into that store again. These three experiences showed me how cultural differences frequently consist of minor, everyday events.

Here is an essay on the same topic. Note that the topic sentence now comes as the last sentence in the introduction. Just as in the first essay, this is the THESIS STATEMENT.

Example 4   Three Cross-Cultural Experiences

    When we think of "culture," we usually think of the customs of special celebrations, as well as such art forms as music, poetry, and painting. I believe that the concept of "culture" also covers everyday life, for example the way people eat, talk, and behave. I have learned a lot about American culture by living with an American family for a month. Three of my experiences in this country stand out in my memory as typically American.

    The first experience was coming down to breakfast at my host family's house on the first day. My host mother had left very early that morning to beat the traffic on her way to work. When I came downstairs, the two children in the family were both sitting in the living room, pouring cereal from a package into their bowls. They didn't even notice me because they were too busy watching TV. In the kitchen, my host father was talking to someone on the telephone. He smiled at me and pointed to the refrigerator, but I didn't understand what he meant and just smiled in return. When he got off the phone, he shouted to the children that it was getting late, and we all rushed out the door. I went to school hungry that day.

The second memorable event was trying to take a shower. Their bathroom is a marvelously big room, but I couldn't figure out how to turn on the water in the shower. There were three knobs above the tub, so I assumed that they were for hot, warm, and cold water. I twisted the "warm" knob, but no water came out. Then I tried the two others, and I did get some water, but it was either too cold or too warm. I was too embarrassed to ask anyone for help with such a simple thing, so after making several unsuccessful attempts, I gave up. I had a cold bath instead, and you can be sure that washing your hair in cold bath water is no pleasure.

The third incident occurred later that week when I went to the supermarket to get some groceries. In my country we always bag our own purchases, so after I had put my food on the counter, I went to the other end of the register, pulled out a bag, and started loading it with my things. Imagine my surprise when an unknown woman came running up to me and grabbed my bag. My first thought was that she was going to steal my food, so I held on tight and said, "This is mine!" Everyone stared at me. When I finally found out what was going on, I was so ashamed that I didn't think I could ever go into that store again.

These three experiences all taught me something about life in the United States. I have learned to be responsible for my own breakfast and lunch, to use the funny equipment such as different showers, and to wait patiently while a store employee bags my food. Learning the ways of another culture is a slow process of adjusting to small differences.

B. YOU'RE IN CHARGE: WRITING TO COMMUNICATE

Below are the introduction and conclusion to an essay and space to write, in outline form, the content of the body paragraphs. The title of this essay is "Three Americans." First, think of how you can support the thesis statement by using examples of three Americans you have met. Then write in the topic sentences of your three body paragraphs. Next, think of *how* you can show what you learned from each of them by events or situations that support each topic sentence. Finally, copy the introduction, write your body paragraphs, and copy the conclusion.

Three Americans

(I. Introduction)

Whenever you go to another country, you learn something about that country's culture. You get to see famous places, and you can listen to the radio and watch TV. However, I believe that you learn most from talking to and observing people. Three Americans that I have met have taught me different aspects of life in the United States.

Canadians

(II. Body paragraph #1)

Topic Sentence: _____

_____

Support:

    a) _____

    b) _____

    c) _____

(III. Body paragraph #2)

Topic sentence: _____

_____

Support:

    a) _____

    b) _____

    c) _____

(IV. Body paragraph #3)

Topic sentence: _____

_____

Support:

    a) _____

    b) _____

    c) _____

(V. Conclusion)

In conclusion, meeting people and talking to them is the best part of traveling to another country. The three people above all showed me something different about American culture, and I will always remember them.

C. PEER HELP WORKSHEET

In the first part of this book, you used Paragraph Checklists to help you learn to revise and edit your own paragraphs. As a way of expanding this idea, you will now use your classmates, or peers, to help you improve your writing while you help them improve theirs.

After you have written your essay about three Americans, exchange it with another student's essay. Read each other's essays and help each other with the rewriting process by using the Peer Help Worksheet below. Return the essay and the worksheet to the writer of the essay.

---

1. *Which American do you think was explained most clearly? Why?*

2. *Organization*

   a. *Does each body paragraph have a topic sentence? If yes, underline the topic sentences and circle the controlling ideas.*

   If no, make a suggestion of an appropriate topic sentence.

   b. *Does each paragraph have sufficient support, in your view? If not, explain why.*

3. *Editing*

   a. *Has each paragraph been indented?*

   b. *Are capital letters appropriately used? Put "cap" above any incorrect usage.*

---

7 The Thesis Statement

A. TOPIC AND CONTROLLING IDEA

The thesis statement is the most important statement in your essay. It is the main idea for the whole essay, and it frequently shows or implies how the essay will be organized. Clear thesis statements are essential for good writing in English.

A thesis statement has two parts: the TOPIC and the CONTROLLING IDEA. The TOPIC is the subject of the essay, what the essay is about. The CONTROLLING IDEA is what you are going to say about the topic. As you can see, this is exactly the same as for topic sentences in paragraphs because the thesis statement in an essay has the same function as the topic sentence has in a paragraph.

As examples of thesis statements, consider those of the three essays in Chapter 6. The topics of the three essays are underlined and the controlling ideas are circled.

1. A personal computer consists of three main components which have different functions. *controlling idea*

 topic

2. Three of my experiences in this country stand out in my memory as typically American. *controlling idea*

 topic

3. Three Americans that I have met have taught me different aspects of life in the United States. *controlling idea*

 topic

It is not enough to just state the topic of the essay although you can often use this as the title of your essay. You must also tell the reader what your essay will say about the subject, which means that you need to have a controlling idea. Here there are many choices. For example, with the topic *personal computer,* you could write thesis statements such as:

1. *A personal computer* is very useful for college students.

(In this essay you would show with examples how a computer can help students in their work.)

2. *Personal computers* can be classified according to the speed of their central processing units.

(In this essay you would show how personal computers fall into different categories according to their types of microchips.)

3. *Brand X of personal computer* gives you more value for your money than *Brand Y.*

(In this essay you would compare the two computers on several points.)

Exercise 1

Underline the topic and circle the controlling idea in the following thesis statements. Can you predict the content of the body paragraphs from the thesis statements?

1. Astronomy is a fascinating science. *No*

2. My two cats are totally different in looks, behavior, and personality. *Y*

3. Soccer is gaining popularity in the U.S. because of the simplicity of the equipment, rules and skills involved. *Y*

4. A study of American history reveals alternating phases of isolationism and expansionism. *50/50*

5. The Civil War occurred mainly due to the economic differences between the North and the South. *50/50*

6. Its beauty, history, and location make Washington, D.C. a fascinating place to visit. *Y*

7. Animal behavior can predict earthquakes. *N*

8. Winter is the best season for sports in Canada. *N*

9. A computer is easy to use if you follow these five steps. *So–So*

10. Black gospel music has greatly influenced several famous rock and roll performers. *50/50*

Needs to be more specific

B. RULES FOR THESIS STATEMENTS

1. A thesis statement must be a statement, not a question.

2. A thesis statement must be a *complete sentence*. This means that it must have a subject and a verb.

3. A thesis statement cannot be a simple statement of fact. A fact does not need any support, and therefore you cannot write an essay about it.

4. A thesis statement must *state* the controlling idea, not just wonder whether or not something is true. This means that you must state your position on the topic; you cannot simply make an announcement of what you are going to do in the essay. *opinion*

5. A thesis statement should have *one* controlling idea, not several different ones.

Exercise 2

Which of the sentences below are thesis statements? Put a check mark next to those that qualify. If a sentence is *not a thesis statement*, write the number(s) of the rule(s) it violates on the line in front of it, and fix it so that it is a thesis statement.

_____ *Y* 1. Japanese cars are better than American cars. *in terms of........*

_____ *N 3* 2. A Mitsubishi is a Japanese car.

_____ *N 4* 3. I am going to show you that seat belts are necessary.

_____ *N 1* 4. Are seat belts necessary?

_____ *N 3* 5. Seat belts save lives and dollars.

N 5 6. Students who work while they are studying meet a lot of people, and their professors also work hard.

N 4/5 7. There are both advantages and disadvantages to working while you are an undergraduate.

Y 8. Work study has more advantages than disadvantages.

N 2 9. Work study: an analysis.

N 4 10. In this essay I will compare working on campus and working off campus.

Exercise 3

Hwk

Now it is your turn to write thesis statements. Imagine that you are going to write essays on the five topics below. Think about *what* you would like to say about your topics and *how* you would like to organize your essays. Then write the five thesis statements.

1. Fast food

   _____

   _____

2. A holiday in your country (specify which one)

   _____

   _____

3. Television programs

   _____

   _____

4. The weather where you are living now (specify the place)

   _____

   _____

5. Popular music

   _____

   _____

Class — Parenting

Political Leader

C. YOU'RE IN CHARGE: WRITING TO COMMUNICATE

Your class will be divided into groups according to your choices of favorite topic from the five topics in Exercise 3. In the groups, brainstorm possible examples, facts, or illustrations that can be used to support each thesis statement. (You will all have different thesis statements, so the exercise involves helping each other and getting ideas from others.) You may change your thesis statement if you decide that another version is better.

After the brainstorming session, organize your material by numbering ideas that go together. These will become the first, second, and third body paragraphs. Cross out any ideas that don't fit. Finally, outline your supporting paragraphs here:

Thesis statement: _____

_____

Body paragraph #1:

Topic sentence #1: _____

_____

    a. _____

    b. _____

    c. _____

Body paragraph #2:

Topic sentence #2: _____

_____

    a. _____

    b. _____

    c. _____

Body paragraph #3: (May or may not be necessary depending on the thesis statement)

Topic sentence #3: _____

_____

    a. _____

    b. _____

    c. _____

Now write your thesis statement as a one-sentence paragraph and add your two or three body paragraphs. (As you know, a complete essay has introductory and concluding paragraphs; however, this exercise does not require a concluding paragraph.) Use good paragraph format.

D. PEER HELP WORKSHEET

Once again, exchange your essay with another classmate's. Fill out the worksheet below to help your classmate with rewriting.

1. *What did you learn from this essay?*

   What did you find most interesting?

2. *Organization*

   a. *Underline the thesis statement. Circle the controlling ideas. Look back at the rules for thesis statements on page 56. Does this thesis statement follow these rules? If not, indicate what needs to be improved.*

   b. *Does each of the body paragraphs support the thesis statement?*

   c. *Are each of the paragraphs unified? Underline any sentences you think are irrelevant.*

3. *Editing*

   a. *Are all the verb tenses correct? Circle any that you think need changing.*

   b. *Are there any spelling mistakes? Put "sp" above any words that are misspelled.*

8 The Introductory Paragraph

The first paragraph in an essay is called the introductory paragraph. Without an introductory paragraph your essay seems too abrupt to an American reader. You need to lead the reader into the subject of the essay. In addition, there is so much written material in the United States that readers will not feel compelled to read what you have written unless you manage to show them in the first paragraph that the essay will be interesting and worth their time to read. As a result, the purpose of the introductory paragraph is two-fold: to introduce the subject of the essay to the readers, and to get their attention.

There are four main types of introductory paragraphs. Let us consider the different ways in which you can introduce the topic "harmful effects of divorce on society."

A. BRIEF ANECDOTE

An anecdote is a short story which illustrates your topic. You can either write this anecdote from your own experience, or you can invent a story concerning someone else. Here are two examples:

Personal Anecdote

My parents divorced when I was in elementary school. This divorce disrupted my childhood and adolescence in serious ways. Indeed, even today it is difficult for me to admit that my parents are divorced. *If divorce has so deeply affected one person, consider the harmful effects divorce must be having on society as a whole.*

Third Person Anecdote

The little girl woke from a nightmare. She ran to her parents' room to see her father so he could comfort her. Then she suddenly remembered that he was no longer living with her. Her parents were divorced. She began to shake and cry. Divorce has greatly affected this child. *Consider the harmful effect divorce seems to be having on society as a whole.*

B. INTERESTING/SURPRISING FACT OR STATISTIC

Another way in which you can introduce your essay is by surprising the reader with facts or numbers. This kind of introduction is especially effective when you have exact figures at your disposal. You can expand your knowledge of facts and statistics by careful reading of newspapers and journals. Here is an example introducing the essay with facts.

> Of every four couples who marry in the United States, one will seek divorce. In some urban areas, the figure is even higher: as many as half the marriages in the Los Angeles area end in divorce. This means that there is an increasing number of single-parent households and of children living without one of their parents. *Consider the harmful effects divorce seems to be having on society.*

C. HISTORICAL INTRODUCTION

You may also choose to write a brief historical introduction to your essay. Naturally, you are not expected to begin with the beginning of time, but you may write a few sentences giving some historical background to your subject.

> One hundred years ago, an unhappy couple simply lived unhappily or tried to work out their problems. Divorce was an option that was never considered. Today, an unhappy couple easily decides that divorce is the answer to their problems. *However, consider the harmful effects these ''easy'' divorces seem to be having on society.*

D. GENERAL TO SPECIFIC

This is perhaps the most common type of introduction. It begins with a general statement of the larger topic and subsequently narrows it down with each following sentence to the thesis statement. Below is an example of such a "general to specific" introduction.

> Any society has many problems. The society in the U.S. is no exception. Some of the problems that the people in the U.S. must deal with are drugs, unemployment, welfare, and the generation gap. However, the basic problem is the changing structure of the family, which causes an overwhelming number of divorces. *Consider the harmful effects divorce is having on the people in the U.S.*

As you can see, all of the above paragraphs could introduce this essay, which would describe in several paragraphs what these "harmful effects" are. In your writing, you should try to develop the skill of writing different types of introductions, so your essays do not become boring and predictable.

Good introductory paragraphs of all types must naturally be relevant to the topic; that is, they should not introduce material not covered in the essay. Secondly, there should be a few sentences before the thesis statement. Finally, an introductory paragraph should not bring up the points which will form the body of the essay.

Exercise 1

Here are two thesis statements introduced by four paragraphs each. In groups or pairs, try to determine which of the four introductions you think are good, which ones not so good, and why you make this decision.

Thesis Statement A

1.   You must plan a party if it is going to be a success. First you need to consider people who are likely to enjoy each others' company, and then you should send out invitations well in advance. In addition, don't forget to have plenty of good music available; people of all ages like to dance. *You can be a great party-giver if you plan in the following way.*

Is this a good introduction?   no

If it isn't, why not?   includes unrelated material for body

2.   Who doesn't like a party? Yet I think everyone has given a party once that just wasn't a success. Great parties don't just happen; they have to be planned, and this takes some time. However, planning a party is worth the time and energy it takes. *You can be a great party-giver if you plan in the following way.*

Is this a good introduction?   Yes

If it isn't, why not? _____

3.   There are all kinds of fun things to do in your leisure time. Participating in sports is probably the most common leisure activity. Sports train your body, teach you to win and lose with a smile, and help you concentrate. For most people, though, being with other people is what they enjoy most. *You can be a great party-giver if you plan in the following way.*

Is this a good introduction?   no

If it isn't, why not?   not related / relevant

4.   Parties are exciting and stimulating. *You can be a great party-giver if you plan in the following way.*

Is this a good introduction?   no   too short

If it isn't, why not? _____

Thesis Statement B

1.   Sports have beneficial effects on your health, but they can also be dangerous. Tennis players develop painful "tennis elbows," skiers break their legs, and careless surfers may drown. *Swimming is the simplest and healthiest sport in which people of all ages can participate.*

Is this a good introduction? _____ no _____

If it isn't, why not? _____

_____

2.   There are all kinds of sports in the world. One distinction we can make is between individual and team sports. Some examples of individiual sports are jogging, swimming, and badminton. Team sports are played by a group of people, usually against another team. In the United States, the best known of all these team sports are baseball, basketball, and football. All these sports are fine, but *swimming is the simplest and healthiest sport in which people of all ages can participate.*

gen to spec.   *gen to spec.*

Is this a good introduction? _____ yes _____

If it isn't, why not? _____

_____

3.   When I was a child, I was quite fat. Our family doctor advised my parents to try to find a kind of sport that I would like so I could get the exercise I needed, but they soon found out that I was too short for basketball, too uncoordinated for tennis, and too slow for track. Then one day my grandmother took me to the local pool and went swimming with me. I loved it! I will never be a competitive swimmer, but I have gone to that pool twice a week ever since and so has my grandmother. *Swimming is the simplest and healthiest sport in which people of all ages can participate.*

anecdote

Is this a good introduction? _____ Yes _____

If it isn't, why not? _____

_____

4.   Finding a sport that you can continue for life is not easy. You need something that doesn't cost much, that requires little equipment, and that won't be too tiring when you get older. I would like to recommend my favorite sport, recreational swimming. In fact, *swimming is the simplest and healthiest sport in which people of all ages can participate.*

not bad

√ informal?

Is this a good introduction? _____ *no contains info for body perhaps*

If it isn't, why not? _____

Exercise 2

Here is a table showing the number of Americans who have died in the wars that the U.S. has fought. Use the statistics from this table to write an introduction to the given thesis statement. Remember that the thesis statement should go at the end of the introductory paragraph.

Thesis Statement

The Civil War was the worst war in U.S. history.

War	No. of Soldiers	Battle Deaths	Percent
Revolutionary War (1775-1783)	250,000	6,824	2.7
War of 1812 (1812-1815)	286,730	2,260	.8
Mexican War (1846-1848)	78,718	1,733	2.2
Civil War (1861-1865)	2,213,363	140,414	6.3
Spanish-American (1898)	806,760	385	.1
WW1 (1914-1918)	4,743,826	53,513	.1
WW2 (1941-1946)	16,353,659	292,131	1.7
Korean War (1950-1953)	5,764,143	33,629	.6
Vietnam War U.S. involvement: (1961–1973)	8,744,000	47,321	.5

Exercise 3

Practice writing introductory paragraphs with one of the following thesis statements. Write at least two introductory paragraphs for the thesis statement you choose. Remember that you can introduce a thesis statement by the use of anecdotes (personal or third person), surprising facts or statistics, historical information, or going from general ideas to specific ones.

1. Japanese cars are better than American cars.
2. A computer is easy to use if you follow these five steps.
3. Washington, D.C. is an interesting place to visit. (Or use a city in your country.)
4. Three experiences in my life have been very frightening.
5. A traditional marriage ceremony in my country is quite fascinating.

Exercise 4

Below is an essay about Diane Sawyer, a broadcast journalist. It does not have an introductory paragraph. Read the essay and then write an appropriate introductory paragraph with a good thesis statement.

Life of a Broadcast Journalist

_____

_____

_____

_____

_____

_____

The first part of Sawyer's career began in Louisville, Kentucky. She worked as a weather reporter and part-time news reporter for a local ABC station. She didn't know much about weather reporting, so she tried to make this part of the news more interesting by reading poems which she thought were appropriate. She liked the news reporting part of her job and tried to do well there, too. All in all, it was a good beginning.

The second part of Sawyer's career took her away from the TV spotlight. She moved to Washington, D.C. and became an assistant to President Nixon. She wrote press releases and speeches for the President. Later on, after Nixon resigned, Sawyer went to California with his staff and helped him write his memoirs. After that project was finished, she moved on.

Next, Sawyer moved back to Washington, D.C. in 1978 and resumed her career as a broadcast journalist. She started to work for CBS News as a reporter. Then, she became a co-anchor of "Morning with Charles Kuralt and Diane Sawyer." This was an early morning news/talk show. Finally, in 1984, she got a job as a reporter on the popular "60 Minutes."

Sawyer has come a long way since her early days at a small TV station. She is now a well-known and respected broadcast journalist. It seems her future can only get better.

E. PEER HELP WORKSHEET

Use this abbreviated worksheet when you exchange your introductory paragraph from Exercise 4 with another student.

1. *What caught your attention in this introductory paragraph? What made it interesting to read?*

2. *Which type of introductory paragraph is it?* (Check one.)

   _____ *personal anecdote*

   _____ *third person anecdote*

   _____ *interesting/surprising fact or statistic*

   _____ *historical introduction*

   _____ *general to specific*

3. *Underline the thesis statement.*

   a. *Is this introductory paragraph revelant to the thesis statement?*

   b. *Check to make sure that the information in the essay is not in the introductory paragraph.*

9 The Concluding Paragraph

The last paragraph of your essay is, of course, the concluding paragraph. This paragraph has a very important function in your essay. It is the last paragraph that your reader is going to read, so naturally you want to leave your reader with a clear understanding of what the point of your essay is. As with concluding sentences, a concluding paragraph can do this in one of two ways.

A. SUMMARY–TYPE CONCLUDING PARAGRAPHS

The first way is to summarize the main points in your essay. You want to remind the reader of each of the ideas that were brought up in your supporting paragraphs. Look at this model essay about New Orleans. Notice the concluding paragraph.

New Orleans: A Unique American City

The United States has many famous cities. In the east, there is New York. With its five boroughs, or parts, it is the largest city in the country. Chicago is the Midwest's largest city and is the center of most forms of transport: road, rail and air. San Francisco and Los Angeles are the big centers of the west. The southern part of the U.S., too, has a business and cultural center in New Orleans. New Orleans is perhaps the most distinctive and interesting city in the U.S.

The people of New Orleans are of a unique mixture of backgrounds. The main group is called Creole. Creole people are pure descendants of French and Spanish settlers. The Cajuns are also French, but they came to New Orleans originally from Canada. Since New Orleans was a slave center before the Civil War, one third of the population is black. Other immigrant groups include Germans, Italians, and Latin Americans. All of these groups make up the distinctive population of New Orleans.

There are some very famous places in New Orleans. New Orleans is perhaps best known as the birthplace of jazz. Preservation Hall on Bourbon Street in the Vieux Carré is famous a gathering place for jazz musicians. The Vieux Carré is also called the French Quarter and is the oldest part of the city. The center of the French Quarter is Jackson Square, which is named for the seventh president of the U.S. and which has a prominent statue of this president. The French Market is an old farmers' market and is still in use today. In short, there are many fascinating places to see in New Orleans.

There are two celebrations in New Orleans each year which draw people from all over the country. The first is Mardi Gras. This is a carnival which takes place before the Christian period of fasting called Lent. On the last day of Mardi Gras, which is also called Fat Tuesday, people dress up in costumes and march in parades or just go to various places to listen to music. It is generally a time for people to go crazy. The second event is called the Spring Fiesta. This celebration is less crazy. It consists of candlelight tours of some of the older and more famous houses in the French Quarter. If you visit New Orleans, you should try to visit during one of these two celebrations.

All in all, New Orleans should definitely be counted as one of the great cities in the United States. Its people are a diverse mixture of many ethnic groups, the Vieux Carré has many interesting sights, and Mardi Gras and the Spring Fiesta, while very different, offer unique celebrations. For all these reasons, New Orleans is a city that highlights the southern part of the United States.

As you can see, the concluding paragraph in this essay mentions each of the main ideas brought out in each of the supporting paragraphs of the essay. This is a summary and one of the ways of writing a concluding paragraph.

B. RESTATEMENT/FINAL COMMENT–TYPE PARAGRAPHS

A second common way of writing a concluding paragraph is to restate the idea of your thesis statement and make your final comment on the subject. Here is an alternate concluding paragraph for the essay on New Orleans. Note how it differs from the summary–type of concluding paragraph.

In conclusion, New Orleans is an important city in the United States, and people should consider it as such. It has a unique atmosphere for business, entertaining or just looking around. Its fascinating combination of old world and new world will make anyone fall in love with it.

The ideas in the thesis statement are repeated in this concluding paragraph.

It is important to notice one point about both kinds of concluding paragraphs. Neither of them bring up new information about the topic of the essay. New information should go in another body paragraph, not in a concluding paragraph.

Exercise 1

Here is an essay about Woody Allen, a famous and funny American who, as you will see, has had many different jobs in the entertainment industry. This essay does not have a concluding paragraph. Read the three choices of concluding paragraphs which follow the essay and choose the best one. Be prepared to explain your answer.

The Many Hats of Woody Allen

America would not be the same without Woody Allen and certainly American humor would not be. Allen has become famous as the neurotic New Yorker who always finds the worst—and the funniest—side of life. He has been tickling the American funny bone for over 25 years. In addition, he has been doing it under many different job titles.

Early in his career, Allen was a "behind the scenes" man. He wrote jokes and ideas for other people to perform. He worked for NBC radio and television performers. Some of the early TV shows in the 1950's, such as Sid Caesar and Garry Moore, had Woody Allen jokes in them. Even though he wasn't a performer, he was gaining valuable experience.

In the early 1960's, while maintaining his writing, Allen became a performer. At first, he was a stand-up comedian. He played to small and large audiences and was even on "The Tonight Show." Later on, he began writing plays and then being an actor in them. One of his most famous plays was *Play It Again, Sam,* which was a neurotic's funny look at Humphrey Bogart's effect on his life. He also began acting in films. In most of these, he was a writer as well as an actor.

In the 1970's, Allen found that he liked another job—directing people in movies. Of course, he never stopped writing or performing. He just added one more job to the overall project of making a movie. One of the most famous movies in which he wrote the screenplay, acted in the lead role and directed was *Annie Hall.* This movie won an Oscar as the best movie of 1977, and Allen won in the same year as best director. He had, indeed, become a success at three different jobs.

a. In conclusion, Woody Allen has been successful and funny at many jobs. He has been a writer for himself and others. He has been a stand-up comedian and an accomplished actor both on stage and in films. One can only wonder about what job Woody Allen will make us laugh with next.

b. In short, Woody Allen is a man of many talents. He can even play the clarinet. He does this every Monday night in a small jazz club in New York. He can also make us laugh by being a writer, actor and director. Americans are lucky to have Woody Allen.

c. All in all, Americans are lucky to have Woody Allen. For more than a quarter of a century, he has been making us laugh by doing what he does best in each of the many jobs he has had. Long live Woody Allen and his sense of humor!

Exercise 2

Here is another essay which does not have a concluding paragraph Write two concluding paragraphs to this essay in the space provided. Make one a summary–type conclusion and the other a restatement/final comment–type of conclusion.

Music, Music Everywhere

As you pull up to a stoplight, you can hear loud music coming from the car next to you. On a street corner, a group of people are gathered around a flute player listening to every song he plays. In a supermarket, shoppers sing along with the muzak in the background. Music is everywhere. In many ways, it is extremely important in people's lives.

People need music in order to relax. After working a long, hard day, people come home upset, tense and at war with the world. All they need to do, however, is to put on some soothing music, and they can't help but become calm. Many relaxing activities, such as lying on a beach or next to a swimming pool, are made more relaxing with music. People even use music to get them into that extreme state of relaxation, sleep.

In addition to needing music for relaxation, music is also necessary for enjoyment. People go to discos and bars every night just to have a good time dancing to their favorite music. Other people get enjoyment from music in more passive ways; they listen to their favorite music at a concert or on the radio or stereo. Still others find pleasure in producing music. These people play musical instruments. In short, people enjoy music in many ways.

The third way in which music is important in people's lives is in bringing them together. People rally around causes or institutions and can identify these causes and institutions by the music that surrounds them. For example, most people are in some way moved to feelings of patriotism upon hearing their national anthem. Many wars have been fought with the aid of a song that can bring soldiers and nations together, assuring their victory. People can even show allegiance to a certain political or social cause by buying and enjoying a particular recording. Music brings people together.

a. SUMMARY–TYPE CONCLUDING PARAGRAPH

_____

_____

_____

_____

_____

b. RESTATEMENT/FINAL COMMENT–TYPE CONCLUDING PARAGRAPH

_____

_____

_____

_____

C. PEER HELP WORKSHEET

Here is another abbreviated worksheet. It focuses on the concluding paragraphs written for Exercise 2.

1. *Which concluding paragraph is the most effective, in your opinion? Why?*

2. *Look at the summary-type concluding paragraph.*

   a. *Does it bring up the main idea of each body paragraph? If not, tell which main idea is missing.*

   b. *Is any new information brought up? If so, underline it. Suggest how it might be eliminated.*

3. *Look at the restatement/final comment-type concluding paragraph.*

   a. *What are the synonyms used to make a restatement of the thesis statement? (Circle them.)*

   b. *What is the final comment of the writer? Is it a reasonable conclusion?*

   c. *Is any new information introduced? If so, underline it. Suggest how it might be eliminated.*

10 Body Paragraphs

A. CONCRETE SUPPORT

The main problem in essay writing is finding the right support to back up your thesis statement. Without sufficient support, an essay becomes VAGUE (too general). American writing is specific. The writer tries to convince the reader with concrete examples, illustrations, and facts, and does not leave the reader to guess what the writer means.

The essay below is vague because the writer hasn't given enough support for a reader to be convinced. Read the essay, look at the facts and statistics following it, and then discuss with a classmate how to improve it.

Charge it!

Almost all Americans use credit cards. Over the last few decades, credit cards have become the most common method of payment for almost anything. I believe that the use of credit cards is a danger to our economy. *because* . . . . .

First of all, credit cards are too easy to get. Since the companies which offer the cards are very big, they cannot check on the financial situation of every person who applies. For this reason, almost any person can get a card whether that person is responsible with money or not.

Secondly, the cards are too easy to use. They are accepted everywhere. There are many places where you cannot use a check, but you can always use your credit card. There are also many times when you absolutely need a credit card, for example when you use the telephone. In addition, you can charge large amounts of purchases on your credit cards since the card companies give you generous credit limits.

Thirdly, you can spread out your payments over a very long time. You don't have to pay the whole amount right away; on the contrary, you only have to pay a little every month. Of course, most of what you pay is the interest that the company charges. In this way, it is easy to buy a lot more than you can really afford, but you don't notice it.

In conclusion, credit cards are dangerous for our economy because people get them too easily, use them too often, and never have to pay off their debts. In this way, many Americans are living beyond their means.

This isn't a bad essay, but it is quite vague, that is, it is very general. It needs more specific facts and examples to make it into a really good essay. On the following pages you will find some statistics and examples that would add more support to the body paragraphs in this essay. Use some of each kind of support (and any other facts or personal examples) to revise the essay and improve its content.

Statistics

Table 1: *Market share of bank issued cards*

VISA	60%
Mastercard	38%
Diners Club	2%

Table 4: *Percentage of households with credit cards*

VISA	53%
Mastercard	44%
American Express	20%
Other cards	10%

(NOTE: These add up to more than 100% because 7 of 10 households have one or more cards.)

Table 2: *Market share of general purpose cards*

VISA	50%
Mastercard	30%
American Express	15%
Other cards	5%

Table 5: *Average yearly interest rates*

VISA	20%
Mastercard	20%
American Express	18%

(no interest if paid in full)
(NOTE: As VISA and Mastercard are issued by banks and other financial institutions, the rates vary.)

Table 3: *Number of major bank cards issued in the U.S.*

VISA	110 mil
Mastercard	66 mil
American Express	33 mil
Other cards	11 mil

Table 6: *Average monthly minimum payment*

VISA	2% of balance
Mastercard	2% of balance
American Express	(paid in full each month)

Interesting credit card facts

- The average American carries 7–8 credit cards (all types).
- The average American family is $10,000 in debt on the total of all its credit cards.
- The total bank card debt in the U.S. was $120 million in 1985.

Examples

Required use of credit cards (by telephone):

1. to reserve a camping space in National Parks

2. to get tickets to concerts through a computer ticket agency

3. to reserve a hotel room

4. to reserve a rental car

5. as deposit for videotape rental (they run a blank form)

6. to order merchandise from catalogs

Cards or cash / cards preferred (no checks):

1. for any purchase out of your state

2. as hotel or rental car payments

Unusual places where credit cards are now accepted as payment:

1. Customs duty

2. Library fines at Denver Public Library

3. Tuition at Mount Saint Mary's College, Maryland

4. Express mail service at post offices in New York City, Dallas, San Diego, Boston, and Norfolk

5. Milwaukee's Yellow Cab Company

6. Bail at Hennepin County Jail in Minneapolis

7. Ski-lift tickets at three Vancouver ski centers

8. Funeral service expenses at Forest Hills, New York

Personal Examples

Your teacher will decide if these questions should be used as an interview assignment or as class discussion.

1. Do you know anyone who has received offers of cards that they already have?

2. Do you know anyone who has used up all the credit on one of his/her cards?

3. Have you ever been in a store where someone asked you to apply for a store credit card? Did anyone try to give you something (a watch, a calculator, etc.) for filling out an application?

4. If you have a checking account, has anyone asked you to show them a credit card in order to accept your check?

5. Can you compare the general interest rate on credit cards with the interest rate of car and home loans in your area?

B. TOPIC SENTENCES AND CONCLUDING SENTENCES IN ESSAYS

In Part I, you learned that individual paragraphs in English start with a topic sentence and end with a concluding sentence. This is usually true for single paragraphs, but it is not always true for body paragraphs in an essay.

There may be times when a topic sentence for each body paragraph is not needed. This can happen when the thesis statement for the essay clearly shows what the topic for each paragraph will be. Consider this thesis statement:

> There are three main differences between New York and Washington, D.C.: population, business and traffic.

caution!

This thesis statement clearly indicates that there will be three body paragraphs in this essay and that they will deal with population, business and traffic in that order. It is important that you, as a writer, maintain the unity of each body paragraph when you choose not to use a topic sentence. Without a topic sentence, it is unity alone that makes a good paragraph.

Yes!

In addition, concluding sentences in body paragraphs sometimes have a different function from concluding sentences in a paragraph. Instead of summarizing the paragraph or paraphrasing the topic sentence, the concluding sentence in a body paragraph may function as a connection, or bridge, to the following paragraph.

Look at the following model essay. Underline the thesis statement. While you read, consider the following questions.

1. Are there any topic sentences?

2. What holds the paragraphs together if there aren't any topic sentences?

3. Are there concluding sentences?

4. What is the purpose of any concluding sentences?

Greenpeace

Do!

The Greenpeace Foundation is an organization which consists of environmentalists from around the world. It began in the early seventies as a response to the increasing disregard for human and non-human life on our planet. Greenpeace primarily fights for the preservation of life against three situations: nuclear testing, whale hunting and seal hunting.

The first major protest of Greenpeace happened at Amchitka. This is a small island in the North Pacific off the coast of Alaska. The United States had been using this area for testing nuclear bombs underground, and another test was scheduled for 1971. The members of Greenpeace decided to invade the waters around the island. They thought that the U.S. would not explode a bomb and take human lives. Unfortunately for Greenpeace, the ships carrying the members to Amchitka were stopped, and the test happened anyway later that year. However, Greenpeace did manage to embarrass the U.S., and, in 1972, it decided no longer to use Amchitka for nuclear testing. Protesting nuclear testing, however, is not all that the Greenpeace Foundation does. *link topic sentence*

Greenpeace also fights against Russian, Japanese and Australian whalers. The first fight happened in 1975 in the North Pacific and was against Russian whalers. Greenpeace volunteers put their ship and themselves between whaling boats and the whales. On this first trip, Greenpeace got the whalers to stop. The Russians decided that they didn't want to kill people as well as whales. Since that first victory, there have been yearly whaling expeditions by Greenpeace to save whales from whalers. Greenpeace's goal is to save whales from becoming extinct.

topic sentence

The Greenpeace Foundation also wishes to save the harp seal from becoming extinct. Norwegian and Canadian seal hunters kill thousands of seals each year in order to get their pelts and sell them. Greenpeace's first seal expedition took place in 1976 off the coast of Newfoundland and Labrador. During this journey, Greenpeace couldn't prevent the killing of 169,000 harp seals, but the workers did get the world's attention. As it does with the whale expeditions, Greenpeace continues to fight against harp seal hunting.

In short, the Greenpeace Foundation has grown to be a true defender of our environment. Since the early 1970's, it has protested in substantial ways against nuclear testing, whale hunting and harp seal hunting. Their greatest victory has been to focus the world's attention on these environmental problems, and, in this way, they have gotten the countries and people responsible to at least slow down their destruction of our environment.

VOCABULARY

expedition = trip
pelt = the fur of an animal
substantial = important in terms of gaining something

C. YOU'RE IN CHARGE: WRITING TO COMMUNICATE

1. Now that you have studied all the parts of an essay, it is time to write a complete essay of your own. Write about a famous city or a famous person in your country. Use information that you already know. Your essay should have five paragraphs: an introductory paragraph, three supporting paragraphs, and a concluding paragraph. Use good paragraph format.

2. The University Application Letter

   You need to do more than fill out an application to get into a college or university. Many times you are also asked to write an essay about yourself, your background, your abilities, and your goals. The university wants this essay both to learn more about you and to see how well you write. Since American universities want their students to have a varied background, they feel that this essay tells them more than just a fill-in-the-blank application.

   Here are some of the basic (minimum) criteria for admission to Green Valley College. Some additional experiences that the college would like to see in its applicants are also listed. Look at the criteria and make notes about yourself in the space provided. Next, make an outline of your essay following the outline suggestions, and finally write the essay.

(This essay is unusual in its organization. The introductory paragraph does not always lead to an explicit thesis statement because it is often inferred from the content of the essay body.)

Basic criteria	You
High school graduate	(school's name, year):
	_____
TOEFL score of 500 or above	(use your imagination): _____
High School GPA of 3.5 or above	_____

GPA = grade point average

Grade point average worksheet

There are usually five American grade levels:
A = 4.0 (top 10% of students)
B = 3.0 (20% of students)
C = 2.0 (40% of students)
D = 1.0 (20% of students)
F = 0.0 (bottom 10% of students)

If your school gave you final grades, try to determine which percentage groups above each grade belonged to. If your school only gave you a diploma and no final grades, follow the worksheet listing your average grade in each of your major subjects.

Subjects:	American grade:	American grade point:
_____	_____	_____
_____	_____	_____
_____	_____	_____
_____	_____	_____
_____	_____	_____
		– – – – – – – – –
Add the grade points and divide by the number of subjects to get your grade point avergage.)		GPA = _____

Experience	You
Paid work	_____
Volunteer work	_____
Leadership positions	_____
Sports	_____
Other	_____
	_____

Now fill in the outline following the suggestions for what to write in each paragraph.

Paragraph 1:
Introduce yourself by briefly describing your family, school, and community. Add a thesis statement which says what you want to do in life.

_____
_____
_____
_____
_____
_____

Paragraph 2:
Describe what you were especially good at in High School. What were your favorite subjects and why?

_____
_____
_____
_____
_____

Paragraph 3:
What extracurricular activities have been most important to you? What qualities about you do these activities show?

_____
_____
_____
_____
_____

Paragraph 4:
What do you want to study at Green Valley College and why? What ideas do you have about your future work? How will your education at Green Valley help you in this?

_____
_____
_____
_____
_____

Paragraph 5:
Write a final comment about
the quality of education at
Green Valley College and your
interest in going there

_____

_____

_____

_____

_____

Now write your essay. Try not to exaggerate your qualities, but don't underestimate yourself either.

D. | **PEER HELP WORKSHEET** |

   After you have finished writing your first completely original essay about a city or person from your country or the university application letter, exchange it with a classmate. Use this worksheet to help each other improve your essays.

> 1. *What did you find most interesting about this essay?*
>
>
>
> 2. *Content*
>
>   *What type of support is used in this essay? Check as many as appropriate.*
>
>   _____ *statistics/facts*
>
>   _____ *examples*
>
>   _____ *personal examples*
>
> 3. *Organization*
>
>   a. *Underline the thesis statement. Circle the controlling idea.*
>
>   b. *How many body paragraphs does this essay have?* _____
>   *Does each have a topic sentence? If yes, underline the topic sentence. If not, is it clear from the thesis statement what the topic of this paragraph is?*
>
>   c. *What is the function of the last sentence in each body paragraph? Is it a true concluding sentence, or is it a bridge to the next paragraph?*
>
> 4. *Editing*
>
>   a. *Is this essay written with good paragraph format?*
>
>   b. *Is the separation between paragraphs clear?*

PART III

Rhetorical Patterns

11 Process

A. MODEL ESSAYS

Read the two essays below carefully:

Model 1

How to Make Taffy

Americans are well known for their hunger for sweet things. They love chocolate, ice cream, cakes, cookies; in fact, they love anything sweet. A traditional American favorite is taffy. Making taffy is very easy if you follow these steps.

First, you need to assemble the ingredients and the equipment. You'll need sugar, corn syrup, cornstarch, butter, salt, and vanilla. You will also need a 2-quart saucepan and a square 8 x 8 inch cakepan. In addition, you will need a candy thermometer. This is a special thermometer that you can put into boiling liquid to register the temperature. You'll also need scissors and some plastic wrap. Now you are ready to start cooking your taffy.

Second, butter the cakepan and set it aside. Mix 1 cup of sugar, ¾ cup of corn syrup, ⅔ cup of water, 1 tablespoon of cornstarch, 2 tablespoons of butter, and 1 teaspoon of salt in the saucepan. Heat the mixture to boiling over medium heat while you stir constantly. Then, cook it without stirring to 256 °F on the candy thermometer. At this point, remove the pan from the heat, and stir in 2 teaspoons of vanilla. Pour the candy mixture into the cakepan immediately.

After you have cooked this mixture, you need to let it cool for about 15—20 minutes. When it is just cool enough to handle, pull the taffy hard with both hands until it becomes shiny, light in color, and stiff. If it gets sticky, butter your hands a little. Pull it into long strips of about ½ inch wide. Cut the strips into pieces with scissors. When you have pulled it like this, wrap each piece in plastic wrap. This is necessary for the candy to hold its shape. When it is completely hard, the final step is easy: eat a piece and enjoy it

As you can see, taffy is a kind of candy that is quite simple to make. It is certainly very sweet, and only for sugar lovers. Moreover, having a taffy-pull party with your friends is every bit as much fun as eating it.

VOCABULARY

ingredients = items needed for making something to eat
to stir = move a spoon in a circular direction
strips = long, thin pieces of something

Model 2

Light Reflection: A Simple Experiment

Why does a balloon go up, but rain falls down? What are shadows? Where do colors come from? Children ask questions all the time, and I enjoy looking for answers with them. There are many simple experiments you can do just by using ordinary items. Here is a quick one showing how light reflects off a mirror.

The equipment you need is right at your fingertips. A mirror on a table, two tubes (the inside of a roll of paper towels, for example), a flashlight, paper, and a pencil are all you need. Stand the mirror against a wall near the edge of the table, and you're ready to start.

First, place the paper on the table in front of the mirror. Then, lay one of the tubes on top of it at an angle to the mirror. It doesn't matter how sharp the angle is, but it can't be perpendicular to the mirror. Now shine your flashlight into the tube at the mirror. Ask a friend to put the other tube on the table next to the first one, and tell him to move it from side to side until he sees the reflected light shining straight at him. It is easier to do this in a dark room, but you should be able to do it anywhere.

Next, draw a line along the right side of the first tube to the mirror, and another line along the right side of the second tube. Take the tubes off the table. What does this show you about light reflection? If you measure the angle between the line to the right and the mirror as well as the angle between the left line and the mirror, you will find that the angles are the same. In fact, you have discovered the angle of light entry to a reflecting source is equal to the angle of its exit.

This science experiment is fun, and it can be a fascinating discovery to a child. It requires very simple equipment, and, as with most science experiments, imagination and an eye for what is going on around you.

VOCABULARY
at your fingertips = close by and easy to get
perpendicular = at a 90 degree angle (⊥)

As you can see, an essay which shows a process is quite similar to an essay that tells a story (narrative). In most of these types of essays, you describe step by step what you do in order to achieve a certain result. To do this well, it is important to make sure that all the steps are covered, and that they are presented in a chronological order.

Exercise 1

1. Underline the thesis statement in both models.

2. What types of introductions are used?

    Model 1:

    Model 2:

3. How are the conclusions organized?

    Model 1:

    Model 2:

Exercise 2

a. Gather some materials with which you can build a small structure on top of a desk. (You can use children's blocks, cuisinere rods, or even books, erasers, and pencils.) Build your "structure," and then make a list of steps for someone to follow to build the exact same structure. The goal of this exercise is for a classmate to be able to build the structure by reading your instructions.

b. Destroy your structure and exchange your instructions and building materials with a class-mate. Build his/her structure while he/she builds yours.

c. Check each other's work. Make any unclear steps in your instructions clear. Add any missing steps.

B. CHRONOLOGICAL LINKING WORDS

As you learned in Chapter 4, *linking words* are those words we use to make a piece of writing hold together as a text. They help connect sentences. Grammatically they are of several different types. They can be *conjunctions* (words that introduce clauses), *adverbs*, *prepositions*, or *transitions*.

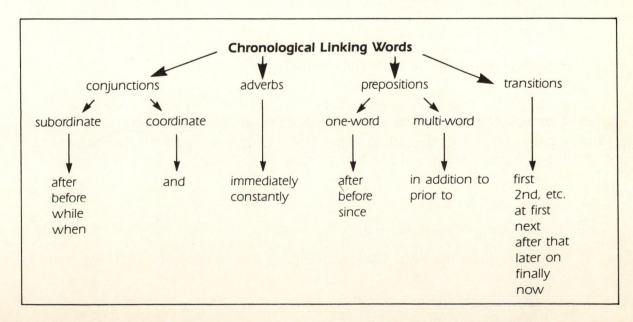

Let us see how they are used in sentences from model essay #1:

1. *First*, you need to assemble the ingredients and the equipment.

2. *In addition to* these items, you'll need a candy thermometer.

3. *Now*, you are ready to start cooking your taffy.

4. *Second*, butter the cakepan and set it aside.

5. Heat the mixture to boiling over medium heat *while* you stir *constantly*.

6. *Then*, cook it without stirring to 256°F on the candy thermometer.

7. *At this point*, remove the pan from the heat, *and* stir in two teaspoons vanilla.

8. Pour the candy mixture into the cakepan *immediately*.

9. *After* you have cooked it, you need to let it cool for about 15-20 minutes.

10. *When* it is just cool enough to handle, pull the taffy hard with both hands *until* it becomes shiny, light in color, and stiff.

Now look at the punctuation used with these linking words.

a) *Subordinator* + dependent clause , independent clause. (Examples: #9 and 10)

b) Independent clause + *subordinator* + dependent clause. (Examples: #5 and 10)

c) *Transition*, independent clause. (Examples: #1, 3, 4, 6, and 7)

d) Preposition *(noun phrase)*, independent clause. (Example: #2)

Exercise 3

Here are 10 steps in the process "How to make scrambled eggs." Copy the sentences using the linking words given in parentheses. Notice that the steps are in the imperative. You will need to change the imperative verbs into present tense verbs when you use conjunctions as linking words.

1. Break 3 eggs into a bowl.

2. Mix them using a wire whisk.

3. Pour in 1 tablespoon of water for each egg.

4. Add a pinch of salt.

5. Heat a frying pan.

6. Melt 1 tablespoon of butter in the pan.

7. Pour in the egg mixture.

8. Stir the eggs by scraping the pan with a spatula.

9. Stop scraping when the eggs are golden yellow.

10. Don't overcook the eggs. Cooking them too long makes scrambled eggs rubbery.

Sentence #1 (first) _____

Sentence #2 (next) _____

Sentences #3 + 4 (after) _____
(Change the imperative verb)

_____

_____

Sentence #5 (at this point) _____

_____

Sentences #6 + 7 (when) _____
(Pay attention to the verb tense.)

_____

_____

Sentences #8 + 9 (until) _____

_____

Sentence #10 (finally) _____

_____

As you have seen, chronological transitions are followed by a comma when they occur at the beginning of a sentence. This is true for *all* transitions. (See Appendix 2 for a list of other common transitions.) The typical pattern is

Independent clause. *Transition*, independent clause.

Another typical pattern is to use a semicolon instead of a period. In this case the pattern is

Independent clause; *transition*, independent clause.

Here are a few examples following this pattern.

1. Your first reason is clear; however, your second is unclear.

2. It is raining today; therefore, my pet snake can't go outside.

3. She tore up all her old love letters; then, she filed for divorce.

Exercise 4

Punctuate the following sentences. Insert commas and semicolons in appropriate places. See Appendix 1 for the punctuation associated with these transitions.

1. After that the Smith family moved to Chicago.

2. Helen doesn't like to go to parties in fact she hardly goes anywhere.

3. First we'll go shopping later on we'll worry about the bills.

4. There are too many cars for the freeway system to handle indeed we are fast approaching gridlock.

5. Furthermore the police can suspend your license.

6. Frank can be very cold in his professional life on the other hand he is very loving with his family and close friends.

7. I don't have enough money in the bank consequently my check will bounce.

8. For example I never do homework.

C. FRAGMENTS

The minimum sentence in written American English consists of a subject and a verb with a tense. The only exception to this rule is an imperative sentence. In the case of an imperative, we say that it has a "hidden subject." Strings of words that either do not have a subject or do not have a verb with a tense are called fragments. Another kind of fragment is a dependent clause that is not connected to an independent clause. The following examples are fragments:

1. Because I needed to buy milk.

2. John singing in the shower.

3. Dancing and laughing on our way home from the party.

4. For example, a shotgun.

Fragments should not be used in academic writing. Here are some ways you can solve the problems with the fragments above.

1. A dependent clause must be connected to a main clause. You, the writer, must decide whether it should be connected to the sentence in front of it or the sentence afterwards. You can write:

I went to the store because I needed to buy milk.

or

Because I needed to buy milk, I went to the store.

2. "Singing" is a verb, but it does not have a tense. There are three forms of the verb in English that do not have a tense: the present participle, the past participle, and the infinitive. "Singing" is the present participle of the verb "sing." To make this fragment into a sentence, you need to change the present participle to a verb with a tense. You can write:

John was singing in the shower.

or

John sings in the shower.

Of course you can also change the sentence to any other tense.

3. This is a fragment because it does not have a subject. In addition, the verb is just a present participle. You need to add a subject and change the verb to a tense form. You can write:

We were dancing and laughing on our way home from the party.

or

We danced and laughed on our way home from the party.

or

Dancing and laughing on our way home from the party, we woke up all the neighbors.

or

another complete sentence

4. This fragment has only a noun phrase ("a shotgun") and no verb. You need to add a verb and to decide if the noun phrase is the subject or object of the sentence. You can write:

For example, a shotgun is used to hunt deer.

or

For example, I think having a shotgun should be illegal.

or

another complete sentence

Exercise 5

In the paragraph below there are six fragments. Find them and correct them.

T-ball

First of all, the equipment. It is very simple. All you really need is a ball, a glove, and a bat. Using the right kind of ball important. A hardball can hurt a child, a softball is too big, but a T-ball designed just for this sport. Make sure that the glove fits the child's hand. Because a glove that is too large will be uncomfortable. There are many kinds of bats on the market. Metal bats, wood bats, even plastic bats. Wood bats are best for this age group. Although they should not do it, children often throw the bat after they get a hit. Another runner may be coming in from third base. And trip over the bat which is lying on the basepath. This can be dangerous. With a T-ball, a good quality glove, and a wood bat the child is ready to play.

D. COHERENCE REVIEW

A list of steps to follow (such as an outline) is made into an text by (1) presenting the steps in the necessary order, and (2) by using transitions to show that order. Below is a process paragraph where the steps are out of order. Organize it so that it makes sense by numbering the steps and write it out in paragraph form.

How to Light a Grill

While the fluid is saturating the charcoal, open the bottom vents of the grill. First, make sure you have enough charcoal. Lighting a charcoal grill is supposed to be a science only men know, but it is really easy if you follow these steps. Heap the charcoal in the grill so it forms a mound. If you have followed these directions, you should now have quite a good fire going. You need to have these vents completely open to get a good fire started. The last step, of course, is to strike a match and hold it at the edge of one of the lower pieces of charcoal. Next, pour starter fluid over the pile of charcoal, and let it soak in for a few minutes.

VOCABULARY
to saturate = to soak (fill up like a sponge)
a vent = an opening
a mound = a small hill

E. YOU'RE IN CHARGE: WRITING TO COMMUNICATE

1. The laboratory report

    a. Here is a series of drawings showing the steps in a simple laboratory experiment. Discuss in small groups what the experiment is trying show, and what the steps in the process are.

    b. Write in:

    1) the point of the experiment: _____

    _____

    _____

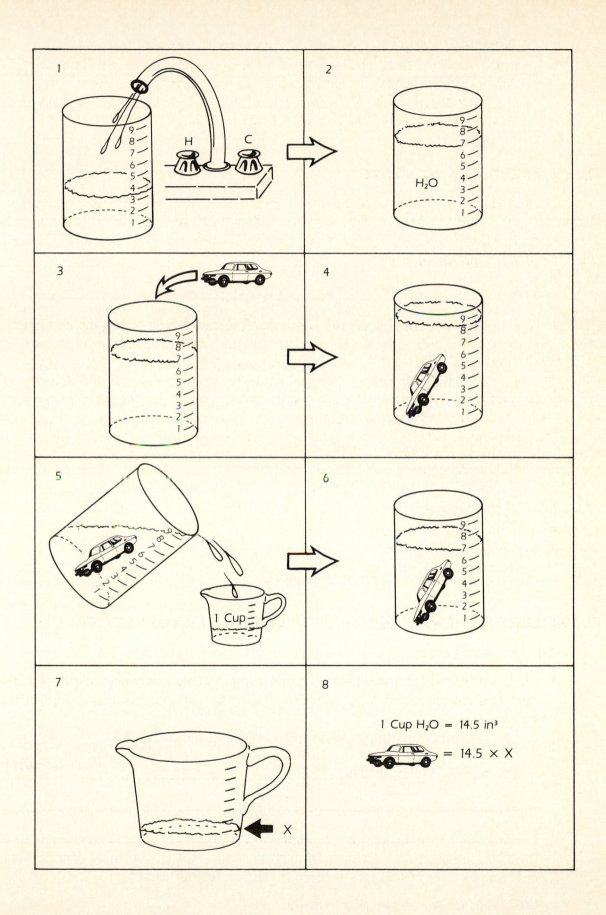

2) the steps:

1. _____

2. _____

3. _____

4. _____

5. _____

6. _____

7. _____

8. _____

   c. After you have decided what the steps are, write a process essay describing this experiment.

2. Preparing for and surviving disasters

Natural disasters can happen anytime, anywhere you live. How can you be well prepared for such a disaster? What could you do before, during, and after to increase your chances of survival? Some possible disasters are listed below. Select one of them.

The West : earthquakes, mudslides
The Mountain areas : avalanches, hailstorms
The Midwest : tornadoes, floods
The South : hurricanes, floods
The Northeast : hurricanes, snowstorms

a. In small groups, brainstorm answers to the following questions:

How can you best prepare for a disaster?

What supplies would you need to survive until help comes? (food, water, heat source, clothes, medical supplies, etc.)

How can you make your house/apartment safer in preparation of a disaster?

What kind of plan should you make to contact other family members or friends?

What should you do and not do during the disaster?

What are the first things to do to recover from the disaster?

b. Compare your answers with another group's answers. Select the best points from both groups.

c. Divide into pairs and discuss how you would organize an essay like this. Make an outline.

d. Consider your introduction to your essay. You want a reader to pay careful attention to what you have to say on such an important subject. Can you think of a personal anecdote or a surprising fact as the introduction to your essay?

e. Write your essay and give it a clear title.

F. PEER HELP WORKSHEET

Here's a Peer Help Worksheet to use when you exchange your essay on a laboratory report or on the preparation for a natural disaster with a classmate.

1. *What did you especially like about this essay?*

2. *Organization*

   a. *Does the essay have a thesis statement with a*

   a) topic _____ ?

   b) controlling idea _____ ?

   If it does, underline it.
   If it does not, suggest a change.

   b. *Does the essay have an introduction? _____*

   What kind? _____

   c. *How many steps are listed in the process? _____*

   Are they in order? _____ yes   _____ no

   d. *Does the conclusion*

   a) restate the thesis? _____

   b) summarize the steps? _____
      or
   c) other? _____

3. *Editing*

   a. *Check the essay for punctuation (run-on sentences, comma splices, fragments, etc.) See Appendix 1.*

   b. *Check the essay for the grammar used with transitions.*

G. OTHER ESSAYS

There is, of course, no limit to the kinds of essays you can write when you are thinking in terms of a process. It can be as long as a book (Dale Carnegie, *How to Win Friends and Influence People*, Pocket Books: New York, 1936), a medium-length article in a magazine ("How to lose 10 pounds in 10 days," "How to succeed in business"), or as short as a list of a few steps. Since you are an academic student, your job is to write an essay about a process. Naturally, your essay

1. All over the world, people play games in their free time. These games can range from simple children's games of jumping rope or playing tag (one person is "it" and runs after the others trying to touch them to make another person "it", and so on), to complex adult games of chess and tennis. Think of a fairly simple game that you know well and write an essay describing how to play that game. Consider the following points:

   a. What equipment do you need?

   b. What are the main rules of the game?

   c. How do you play the game to win?

2. Since you have studied at least one foreign language (English) for a long time, you are in a sense an "expert" on the subject "How to study a foreign language." Think about your experiences in studying English and talk to others about what they have done. Then write an essay giving advice to another person on what to do to be successful in learning a foreign language. Remember that this should be a process of steps to follow in studying. Think about these points:

   a. What can you do to learn to understand the spoken language?

   b. What can you do to practice speaking it?

   c. How can you best remember all the new words you learn?

   d. How can you increase your understanding of the written language?

   e. How can you become a better writer?

3. Try to write a funny essay where you describe the opposite of what people usually want. Some examples are:

   How to fail a test
   How to gain 50 lbs.
   How to be a boring person
   How to make a lot of enemies

When you finish writing your essay, exchange it with a classmate's. See Appendix 3 for a General Peer Help Worksheet.

12 Classification

A. MODEL ESSAYS

Read the two essays below carefully.

Model 1

Learning Styles

When I was in high school, I had to write down everything in order to learn it. I was jealous of my friend Martha who seldom wrote anything down but who learned everything better than I did. I always wondered why this was so. Later, in college, I learned that people simply have different learning styles. In fact, there are three distinct styles of learning: visual learners, auditory learners, and kinesthetic learners.

Visual learners need to see words, diagrams, charts, outlines, or pictures in order to truly understand and remember the material. These people remember a page in a book like a photograph. One example of a visual learner is my friend Annette. Annette is a biology student, and she has to listen and take notes to long lectures in her field. The way she remembers the lecture material is by transforming her notes to diagrams when she gets home. A line drawing or a diagram tells her more than pages and pages of text. For a visual learner, this is the best way to study.

The second type of learner is the auditory learner. This kind of person needs to hear words or sounds in order to master new material. For a student like this, silent reading is not the best way to learn, but he or she will be excellent at following oral directions. Hiroshi, for instance, is an auditory learner. He always asks the teacher to record words and sentences, sometimes whole pages, on his tape recorder. At home, he listens to the tape over and over. As a result, his pronunciation is the best in the whole class. A person with this learning style should make sure to recite everything he studies so he can listen to his own words.

Finally, there are the kinesthetic learners. People with this learning style like ''learning by doing.'' Sometimes they learn best by manipulating objects, moving around, or doing role-plays. My friend Mohammed is a good example. He is a wonderful piano player, and he says that he learns English by pretending that grammar rules are laid out on a piano keyboard. To remember one of them, he often moves his fingers up and down on the desk. He ''plays'' English as he plays the piano. Kinesthetic learners especially enjoy laboratory classes since they can use their whole bodies in learning. To study effectively, they should try to act out the material they are learning.

In conclusion, while most people use a combination of these three styles, one style may work best for one individual. In addition, students may do better in school if they figure out which style works best for them and then adapt their studying method to that style.

VOCABULARY
to be jealous = to think that other people are luckier than you are
to transform = to change
oral = spoken
to manipulate = to use your hands
to recite = to say aloud

Model 2

A Typical Orchestra

Most people can identify some of the instruments of a typical orchestra, and most agree that there are basically four types. These four categories have traditionally been identified in the same way that the composer Haydn did in the 18th century: string, woodwind, brass, and percussion instruments. However, there is another way to classify instruments in an orchestra. They can be divided into four other groups according to the way in which their sound is produced.

The first group is called chordophones. This word comes from ''chorda'' which means strings in Latin and ''phone'' which means sound in Greek. Knowing this, it's easy to realize that chordophone instruments are the string instruments. Strings are placed over a hollow box, and then they are plucked or vibrated with a bow. Examples of these kinds of instruments are violins, cellos, and guitars.

Aerophones make up the second group. If you know that ''aer'' means air in Greek, you can figure out that these instruments make their sound with air. This group includes two of the traditional groups, woodwinds and brasses, since both of these types of instruments make their sound by air being blown through a tube. The tube may be straight as in flutes or clarinets, or it may be curved as in trumpets or tubas. Other examples of aerophones include piccolos, trombones, and cornets.

Thirdly, there are the membranophones. The Latin ''membrana'' means skin, so membranophones are those instruments which have skins covering a hollow bowl of some kind. Of course, we usually call these instruments drums. The skin vibrates when it is hit with a stick or by hand, and the bowl works like an amplifier. Traditionally, drums like the timpani, kettledrum, bass drum, and tom-tom make up part of this percussion group of instruments.

The fourth group of instruments makes up the other part of traditional percussion instruments. These are the idiophones. ''Idios'' comes from Greek and means personal or separate. This is a little more difficult to figure out, but idiophone instruments basically vibrate by themselves separately. Their sound is not produced by strings causing resonance in a box as with the chordophones, by air vibrating in a tube as with the aerophones, or by a box set in motion by a strike on a membrane as with the membranophones. Idiophones are such instruments as the triangle, gong, bells, or cymbals.

In conclusion, we can classify the instruments in a orchestra according to the way the sound of the instrument is made. In addition, by knowing a little Latin and Greek, we can easily understand these four groups: chordophones, aerophones, membranophones, and idiophones.

VOCABULARY
to pluck = to pull on a string with your fingers and then let it go
resonance = echo (vibrating air)

Classifying, or dividing something into classes or categories, is a natural function of human beings. We do a lot of classifying in our daily lives. We divide movies into good and bad ones, we say that people are friendly, neutral, or unfriendly, and we classify cars into subcompacts, compacts, mid size, and full size ones. It is important to note that we always classify according to a PRINCIPLE, even though we may not be aware of it. If we want to write an essay which classifies, we must state the GROUP we are classifying (e.g. cars) and the CATEGORIES (e.g. subcompacts, compacts, etc.) that are the result of the classification in the thesis statement. In addition, we frequently state the principle of classification in the thesis statement. It is important to note that the categories need to be MUTUALLY EXCLUSIVE. This means that two items cannot belong to the same category at the same time. For example, no car can be both a subcompact and a compact.

Look at the diagram below. It explains the meaning of the concept MUTUALLY EXCLUSIVE:

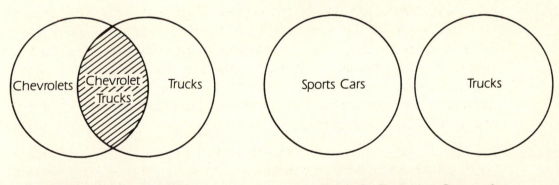

Overlapping Categories   **Mutually Exclusive Categories**

Now look at the table below. Can you think of other categories?

Group	Principle	Possible Categories	
		#	Names
buildings	use	6	office, residential, manufacturing, schools, arts, storage
housing	ownership	2	owned, rented
dishes	cooking methods	5	boiling, broiling, baking, frying, barbequeing
pets	species	4	mammals, reptiles, birds, fish (insects?)
writing	reading pattern	4	right to left, left to right, top to bottom, wrap-around ( )
books	truth	2	fiction, non-fiction

Exercise 1

Look at the table below. How many principles and categories can you think of for the group "people?"

Group	Principle	Category	
		#	Names
people			

Exercise 2

Are the categories in the thesis statements below mutually exclusive? Write OK under the thesis statements where the categories do not overlap (that is, they *are* mutually exclusive), and explain what is wrong with the other thesis statements.

1. Cars come in all colors: red, green, blue, and sports cars.

2. Some people are rich, some are happy, and some are poor.

3. Musicians can be divided into two categories: composers and performers.

4. Painting, sculpture, music, and writing are forms of art.

5. Countries can be classified according to their political systems into monarchies, republics, or dictatorships.

Exercise 3

Look back to the table and Exercise 1. Write thesis statements following this example:

Example: books

> Books can be divided into the two main categories, fiction and non-fiction, on the basis of their truth value.

(NOTE: Look at Exercise 2 for examples of possible sentence structures for these thesis statements.)

1. buildings

_____

_____

2. housing

_____

_____

3. pets

_____

_____

4. people

_____

_____

5. people

_____

_____

B. INTRODUCTORY PARAGRAPHS FOR ESSAYS WHICH CLASSIFY

Imagine that your assignment is to classify the group "human food" into categories according to the principle "origin," that is, where the food comes from. The categories will be:

1. plant food (fruit, vegetables, grains, etc.)

2. animal food (meat, chicken, fish, etc.)

3. animals products (milk, eggs)

Exercise 4

Read the introductory paragraph below. What kind of an introduction is it? Now write *another* introduction to the same essay, using the same thesis statement. Your introduction should be of the "general to specific" kind. (See Chapter 8.)

Food Groups

I know a little boy who will only eat four things: peanut butter sandwiches, yogurt, hot dogs, and scrambled eggs. The only thing he will drink is apple juice. His mother has been battling with him since he was one year old to try to get him to eat other dishes, but without success. He simply refuses. One time he didn't eat anything for three days because she wouldn't give him those things. Now, however, she doesn't worry anymore; her son is really getting what he needs! He is eating something from each of the major food groups, and he is not going to die of malnutrition. These major food groups are: plant food, animal food, and animal products.

Write your introduction here:

_____

_____

_____

_____

_____

_____

_____

_____

_____

C. SUPPORTING PARAGRAPHS IN ESSAYS USING CLASSIFICATION

You may think that one sentence is enough to complete your classification, so how can this become an essay? As usual, the skill lies in choosing detailed examples and descriptions to convince your reader that your categories are reasonable. For example, let's say that you have divided the group "my friends" into three categories: the worrywarts (people who worry all the time about everything), the bookworms (people who study all the time), and the fatalists (people who feel that life is outside their control). It is your thesis that all of your friends fall into one of these three groups. Now, however, you need to show your reader exactly what makes the people in one group different from those in the other two. To do this you think: "How does a worrywart act? How does this person feel and behave in certain situations where the others would feel and behave very differently? How do I feel when I am with a person like this?" When you think about it, perhaps each kind of person brings out different aspects of you when you are with them, and that's why you have chosen them to be your friends.

Exercise 5

Discuss in groups what people do in these situations:

1. It's 8 A.M., and the writing class starts at 8:30 A.M. The bus should have left at 7:45 A.M., but it's late, and your friend won't get to class on time. What would this person do?

   a. a worrywart:

   b. a bookworm:

   c. a fatalist:

2. Your friend was in a car accident. He wasn't hurt badly, but the insurance company says it was his fault, and it won't pay for the damages to his car. What would this person do?

   a. a worrywart:

   b. a bookworm:

   c. a fatalist:

3. The International TOEFL Test is two weeks from now. Your friend must get a score of 500 to be accepted to the college she wants to go to. What would this person do?

a. a worrywart:

b. a bookworm:

c. a fatalist:

D. LINKING WORDS

In essays which classify, the use of such linking words as transitions, phrases, or adverbs of EXAMPLE is crucial. In order for your reader to clearly grasp how you are classifying, you need to give at least one example of each category. In addition, you will frequently want to use linking words of CONSEQUENCE in the concluding sentence of a paragraph to summarize for your reader how your examples relate to your classification principle. Look at these examples below.

Linking Words for Examples

for example
> Some of my friends are introspective and quiet people. *For example,* Ching and Hirofumi never say much when we are together with other people.

for instance
> Rural people are quite different from urban people. My uncle, who is a farmer, is never in a hurry. Once, *for instance,* he spent the whole day sharpening all the knives in the house, a task that an impatient city person would have taken care of in an hour.

another example is
> One such metropolis is Mexico City. *Another example is* Rio de Janeiro.

Linking Words of Consequence

therefore
> I really enjoy the peaceful company of good friends. *Therefore,* the relaxed calm of both Carlos and Maria is a quality I appreciate in a friend.

for this reason
> Change makes life exciting; *for this reason,* life in a city is more desirable than life on a farm or in the suburbs for me.

as a result/consequence
> The poverty of the barrio is not that different from the poverty of the ghetto. *As a result,* urban improvement through city planning alone is practically impossible.

consequently
> Fuel economy has come to be an essential aspect in choosing a car. *Consequently,* smaller and more efficient cars sell better today than they did 20 years ago.

Exercise 6

Combine the two ideas below with a linking word of EXAMPLE or of CONSEQUENCE. Watch your punctuation!

Example: sunny day — go swimming

It was a sunny day. Therefore, we went swimming.

1. miserable weather — cancel picnic

   _____

2. solar energy — heat water

   _____

3. an ordinary bird — canary

   _____

4. being sick — going to the doctor

   _____

5. calling home — being homesick

   _____

6. Southwestern state — Arizona

   _____

7. being in love — getting married

   _____

8. living U.S. ex-presidents — Jimmy Carter

   _____

9. too much work — not going to a party

   _____

10. dangerous sport — American football

    _____

E. PUNCTUATION RULES: THE COMMA

1. In Lists:

In English writing, we usually put commas between all words in a list of more than two items.

Examples:

There are three kinds of teachers: good, bad, and indifferent.

We can divide means of transportation according to the type of energy used: human energy, natural energy, fossil fuel, and nuclear power.

Would you like coffee, tea, or a soft drink?

2. In Adverbial Clauses:

When a sentence begins with an adverbial clause, there must be a comma between this clause and the main clause.

Examples:

Because libraries must organize their books, they have created a system of classification.

If we look at the types of books in a library, we will see that there are three main kinds.

Although an almanac isn't frequently used, it is still a reference book.

3. With Coordinating Conjunctions:

As you learned in Chapter 11, there is always a comma between the two independent clauses connected by a coordinating conjunction. You can remember the seven coordinating conjunctions by using the word "FANBOYS."

F = for
A = and
N = nor
B = but
O = or
Y = yet
S = so

When these words are used to connect sentences, they are preceded by a comma. Although they can technically come in the beginning of a main clause after a period, it is not considered good style to use them in that position.

Examples:

For breakfast he eats cold cereal, or he just drinks a cup of coffee.

They have plenty of money to buy food, yet they are still unhealthy.

There are three major food groups, and it is important to eat a little of each of them.

Exercise 7

Add commas to this paragraph. It is the second supporting paragraph of a classification essay on pets.

Another kind of pet is the caged one. There are three main kinds of caged animals: birds reptiles and rodents. Because they are colorful and graceful to look at birds are very popular. In my country some people have only one big bird in a cage but others have several small ones fluttering and chirping around in a single cage. I would never consider having a reptile such as a snake in my house but a friend of mine has a boa constrictor in a cage in his bedroom. He says that it is a lovely pet since it doesn't bark doesn't eat much and never needs to be taken out for a walk. Rodents are small furry cute animals like guinea pigs gerbils and hamsters. They are especially popular with children. If they are treated properly they can live quite a long time in their cages. Caged animals have a fascination for people who mostly like to watch their pets.

F. YOU'RE IN CHARGE: WRITING TO COMMUNICATE

1. Sports

a) Sports can be classified according to many principles. One principle could be the number of players needed. Another principle might be the equipment necessary. How many other principles can you think of to classify the group "sports?"

PRINCIPLES:

_____   _____

_____   _____

_____   _____

_____   _____

b) Now pick one of your principles above and write down the categories of sports following that principle (at least two categories):

PRINCIPLE: CATEGORIES:

_____   _____

                               _____

                               _____

                               _____

c) What examples of sports can you give for each of your categories? What is special about each of these sports?

CATEGORY 1:   EXAMPLES:

_____   _____

                                                                _____

                                                                _____

CATEGORY 2:   EXAMPLES:

_____   _____

                                                                _____

                                                                _____

CATEGORY 3:   EXAMPLES:

_____   _____

                                                                _____

                                                                _____

d) Write the first draft of your essay. Try to create an interesting introduction and make sure your thesis statement is clear.

2. What on Earth?

Your whole class is a space exploration team which has been captured by the natives of the planet Ohm. The Ohmians have never seen beings like you before, and in order to let you escape, they demand that you classify the inhabitants, biology, and structure of your home world for them. You have been divided into groups of three people, and each group has been given a different task. The Ohmians are planning to visit earth, and if they find that you have lied to them, the whole team will be executed. They have put only one restraint on you: your classification must contain no more than *five* categories. You have 15 minutes to come up with an answer.

Group 1: land animals
Group 2: sea animals
Group 3: physical differences in people
Group 4: mental differences in people
Group 5: political systems
Group 6: communication methods
Group 7: energy sources
Group 8: plant life
Group 9: economic systems
Group 10: family groups
Group 11: clothing
Group 12: educational systems

Present your classifications to the class. They will try argue that your categories are not mutually exclusive or that you have missed something. Listen to what they say, and, if you need to, change your categories or add other examples.

Write an essay based on the classification you have done. After you have finished, exchange the essays and read the other two essays from the people in your group. Discuss the differences and similarities between the essays. Finally, rewrite your essay and hand it in.

3. Classification by Appearance

Below is a group picture. In small groups, try to classify the people in it into no more than three categories. Any classification which divides the whole group into two or three categories with no overlapping is acceptable. Describe each category as completely as you can. Imagine that your reader will not be able to see the picture. Therefore, you have to use all your skills of *description* to convince this reader that your classification is reasonable. After the discussion, outline an essay based on your conclusions. Finally, write your essays on a separate piece of paper.

4. Information for Tourists

Pretend that you work for a travel bureau in your home town. You want to write a travel brochure for American tourists. Your home town has many attractions: its people, food, buildings, scenery, art, etc. In this assignment, you should try to classify these attractions.

a) Individual brainstorming

List all the things that are wonderful about your home town. This list does not have to have any order. Just write down anything that comes into your head as you think about your special town.

b) Organization

Look over your list. Group all the things that should come in the same paragraph by numbering them 1, 2, 3, etc. according to which body paragraph that item will appear in. Will you have too many paragraphs? Perhaps you will want to shorten the list by cutting out one or two points.

c) First draft

Write your first draft and put it away for a while. Then pull it out again and reread it. Is it clear to someone who has never seen you home town? If you think it may not be, revise it accordingly.

d) The introductory paragraph

You may want to use this paragraph to describe the location of your town. However, make sure that your introduction does not include the points that you want to use in the essay.

e) Rewriting

After you have revised and edited your essay, rewrite it and hand it in.

G. PEER HELP WORKSHEET

This Peer Help Worksheet focuses on the essay using classification as a rhetorical pattern. Use it when you read your classmate's essay.

> 1. *What did you find most interesting about this essay?*
>
> 2. *Organization*
>
>   a. *How many body paragraphs does this essay have?* _____
>
>   b. *Does the thesis statement show that there will be this number of paragraphs?*
>
>   Circle: YES   or   NO
>
>   c. *Does each paragraph describe <u>one</u> category?*
>
>   Circle: YES   or   NO
>   *If the answer is NO, write what you think is the problem here.*
>
>   d. *Is there a conclusion?*   YES   NO
>
>   e. *If there is a conclusion, what kind is it?*
>
> 3. *Editing*
>
>   a. *Spelling: Underline all words that are misspelled. Use a dictionary.*
>
>   b. *Punctuation: Read each of the sentences carefully to check the use of all commas. Circle any commas you think are incorrect.*

H. OTHER ESSAYS

Look around you. Almost anything can be classified: trees, animals, chemicals, theories of government, and so on. Below are suggestions for other essays in which you classify a group into categories. Remember that giving concrete support by way of examples is very important in order to convince your reader of your classification. Try to be as original as you can in your classifications to make the writing interesting both for you and for your reader.

1. Look in a local newspaper for a listing of movies playing near you. You may also want to look for movie reviews in newspapers and magazines or go to see a couple of them. Write an essay classifying the group "local movies" into categories according to a principle (e.g. quality of acting, movie type, or popularity). Use the titles of the movies as examples to support your classification and explain a little about each of the ones you use.

2. The number of jobs people can have seems endless, but there are common features in many of them. Think of the group "jobs" and try to classify it into a manageable number of categories—no more than five or six. Start by listing all the types of jobs you can think of; then see if you can divide those into categories. What is your principle of classification?

3. Every country has a political system of organization; however, they also differ in the way their governments are set up. Think about and list countries and their political systems. When you look at your list of countries, can you see a way of dividing them into categories? Your principle here is "political system." How many categories do you find?

13 Comparison and Contrast

A. MODEL ESSAYS

Read the model essays below.

Model 1

A Tale of Two Cities

"Where do you come from?" is a question many Americans can't answer. So many Americans were born one place, lived a few years in another, went to elementary school in a third town, and so on. In my native country, we usually live in the town where we are born all our lives, but my family is different. We moved from one small town to another when I was 12 years old. For this reason, I have two "home towns." Although the inhabitants of the two towns think that they have nothing in common, in my opinion, they have far more similarities than differences.

The first obvious similarity lies in the location of the two cities. They are both seaside towns, lying on the south coast of Norway. They are sheltered by a large group of islands and backed by hills that cover them from the cold winter winds. There are a few minor differences in their location, of course: Kristiansand, my childhood city, spreads out onto many of the protecting islands, while Arendal, my teenage town, needs all the cover it can get from its islands.

Secondly, both Kristiansand and Arendal are small. Compared to the great continental cities of Paris and Rome, they are not even dots on a map. Kristiansand is a little larger with 40,000 inhabitants, while Arendal has only about 35,000, but neither can be called a metropolis.

Furthermore, at least to a visitor, they are quite similar in their natural beauty. The islands are rough and rocky. The houses of both towns are mostly small wood structures painted white, and the vegetation is almost exactly the same: birches, a few fir trees, low bushes, and moss. In addition, the ocean influences the lifestyle of both towns, and the weather forecast is the major topic of conversation.

The economics of the two towns is also based on the same business: tourism. Both native Norwegians and foreigners go on summer vacation to the two cities, and in winter, business is very slow. Of course, there are a few differences here as well. In Arendal, there are still several fishermen making a living from the sea, while Kristiansand is a busy port for large commercial ships. Still, I doubt that either city could support the population it has without the tourists.

point by point.

Finally, despite the opinions of the natives of Kristiansand and Arendal, I think that the people there are very similar. Because of the size of the towns, people are mostly interested in what their neighbors do and say, and they don't care very much about what is happening in the big world. In addition, the inhabitants of the two towns have a love-hate relationship with the necessary tourists. These tourists bring in business and money in the summer, so the natives smile at them when they meet them. However, behind their backs, the towns-people wish that they would spend their money and go home.

Thus, while there *are* a few differences between Arendal and Kristiansand, I think that the similarities are by far more obvious. In location, size, scenery, business, and inhabitants they are very much alike. Although I sometimes feel they are too small for me, they are my home towns, and there is no place like home.

VOCABULARY

a native country = the country where a person was born
an inhabitant = a person who lives in a country or city
to have nothing in common = to have no similarities
location = place
to be sheltered by = to be protected by
a metropolis = a large city
vegetation = plants
a birch = a tree with a white trunk and small, light green leaves
a fir tree = a tree with needles which it does not lose in winter
moss = soft grass-like ground-covering which feels like a sponge
to make a living from = to get their income from
a port = a harbor (where big ships can dock)

Model 2

My Two Sisters

My grandfather, who was interested in genealogy, once traced our family tree as far back as he could, but he couldn't get further back than to 1759. In that year a ship of unknown origin visited our little town, and nine months later a baby boy was born to the only daughter of the small fishing family from which our family came. No one knows what nationality that sailor was, but the genes he passed on have been playing tricks with our solid family ever since. In every generation someone shows up who is radically different from all the others. In my generation, it's one of my sisters, Lisa, who is different. Lisa and Ellen, who is my other sister, are as opposite as night and day.

Lisa, who typifies the night side of the family, is my older sister. Lisa is tall, slim, and elegant, with long, dark hair and brown eyes. She looks tanned even in winter and is always the first person in spring to start wearing shorts. Her personality fits her looks. When Lisa gets angry, she doesn't just do it in a small way; she blows up so loudly that it can be heard in the next town. When she's happy, she's ecstatic. When Lisa found out that she had passed her university entrance exam, she danced in bare feet through the whole town and partied for two solid weeks. She is always on the lookout for new and exciting experiences, and she never does anything halfheartedly. Her passion for life extends from love to politics; she's divorced with three daughters by two different husbands and a dedicated socialist. There's nothing ordinary about Lisa.

Ellen, my younger sister, is her exact opposite. Where Lisa is tall and dark, Ellen is short (5 feet 2 inches) and blond. Lisa wears her hair long and swinging, but Ellen has no time for such nonsense and wears her blond hair in a short and unfussy style. Ellen's eyes are summer-sky blue, clear and untroubled. In summer, Lisa tans, but Ellen gets sunburned easily, and always carries bottles of suntan lotion for herself and her equally blond children. Ellen is as calm as Lisa is excitable. I have never yet heard her raise her voice at anyone, and her laugh is a gentle breeze in contrast to Lisa's gale. Unlike Lisa, Ellen has never changed husbands, nor does she have any intention of doing so. On her wedding day, Ellen smiled softly and dressed in a traditional white dress. Lisa, on the other hand, wore a red mini-dress at her first wedding and blue jeans at her second. Ellen is a summer day, a calm ocean. She devotes herself entirely to her children and her home. Visiting Ellen's house is like coming home.

How can two such opposites be born to the same family? Until genetic research can come up with an answer, I am content to believe the story of the unknown sailor. In fact, even if a scientist should find the real answer, I'd rather not know. Some things are more interesting when left in the dark.

VOCABULARY

genealogy = the study of a family's history
to trace = to follow back through history
to blow up = to get very angry
ecstatic = very happy
halfheartedly = doing something with only half your effort
unfussy = easy to deal with; not bothersome
a gale = a strong wind

Model 3

Community Colleges and Universities

After a student finishes high school, he or she has many choices. The student can try to get a job, start vocational training, or pick a college or university for further study. Community colleges and universities have some differences, but for the most part they are similar.

The first difference is the length of study in the two schools. A community college usually offers only two years of instruction, while a university has both four-year undergraduate programs and graduate studies. Unlike universities, community colleges have special two-year programs leading to an Associate degree. You can, for example, study nursing, airplane mechanics, fashion design, or

Block Style #1.

liberal arts in such a program. In addition, the classes are usually smaller at community colleges than at universities, and the atmosphere is less competitive. Community colleges are also different from universities in the amount of counseling they give new students. You will find more people trained in helping you to make your choices at a community college than at a university.

However, while they do have some differences, the two types of schools have many more similarities. First of all, they both offer two years of undergraduate, general education courses. In fact, with the help of a counselor, you can take almost exactly the same classes at a community college as at a university. With an Associate degree from a good community college, you should be able to transfer with most of your credits to a four-year university where you can complete your Bachelor's degree in two additional years. Furthermore, many community colleges have a campus-like setting, just as most universities do. Students are as serious as students anywhere else, and you will find the library equally crowded at a community college as you will at a major university. In addition, the quality of the instructional staff is high at both types of schools. With the current intense competition for teaching jobs, community colleges are able to attract just as well qualified teachers as universities. Finally, teaching methods are fairly much the same at both schools: lectures, seminars, and laboratory work.

Which school is right for you? The answer depends on your plans for the future. If you are convinced that a professional school (law, medicine, etc.) is the only place for you, then you should probably pick the most famous university you can get into. On the other hand, if you haven't completely planned out your life and you need some more time to think before you commit yourself, you may find that a community college serves your needs very well.

VOCABULARY

atmosphere = general feeling

competitive = when people try to win something

to counsel = to give advice

to transfer = to change to another school

intense = strong

to commit yourself = to make a decision

There are basically three ways of organizing essays which use the comparison and contrast rhetorical pattern. They can be described in this way: Two things (ideas, objects, people, systems, etc.) are compared. We will call them "X" and "Y."

1. Block Style #1

I. Introduction with thesis statement

II. Body paragraph 1: Describe X

   A. point 1
   B. point 2
   C. point 3
   D. point 4
      Etc.

III. Body paragraph 2: Describe Y with reference to X
    A. point 1 : Y vs. X
    B. point 2 : Y vs. X
    C. point 3 : Y vs. X
    D. point 4 : Y vs. X
        Etc.

IV. Concluding paragraph

2. Block Style #2

I. Introduction with thesis statement

II. Body paragraph 1: similarities of (or differences between) X and Y
    A. first similarity
    B. second similarity
    C. third similarity
        Etc.

III. Body paragraph 2: differences between (or similarities of) X and Y
    A. first difference
    B. second difference
    C. third difference
        Etc.

IV. Concluding paragraph

3. Point by Point Comparison

I. Introduction with thesis statement

II. Body paragraph 1: first point of comparison
    A. X
        1. example of X according to point 1
        2. example of X according to point 1
    B. Y
        1. example of Y according to point 1
        2. example of Y according to point 1

III. Body paragraph 2: second point of comparison
    A. X
        1. example (point 2)
        2. example (point 2)
    B. Y
        1. example (point 2)
        2. example (point 2)

IV. Body paragraph 3: third point of comparison
   A. X
      1. example (point 3)
      2. example (point 3)
   B. Y
      1. example (point 3)
      2. example (point 3)

(There may be more body paragraphs.)

V. Concluding paragraph

In both block styles, we have shown four body paragraphs. (There can, of course, be more depending on the length and detail of the essay.) An essay written in Block style #1 will usually have a longer second body paragraph than the first body paragraph because this is the paragraph where most of the comparison takes place. Similarly, in Block style #2, you need to decide whether the similarities or the differences are more important. The body paragraph that contains most of the comparisons from the controlling idea in the thesis statement will be longer than the first body paragraph. In a point-by-point comparison, there will be as many body paragraphs as there are points on which the two things are compared.

Exercise 1

Which method of organization is used in each of the three model essays?

Model 1:

Model 2:

Model 3:

B. LINKING WORDS

As with chronological linking words (See Chapter 9), comparison and contrast words are of the four types: *conjunctions*, *prepositions*, *adverbs*, and *transitions*. Below are examples of their use in comparing the two imaginary towns: "Stonecreek" and "Linden."

Showing Differences

Conjunctions (subordinators)

1. Stonecreek is small, *whereas* Linden is large.

2. *While* Stonecreek is small, Linden is large.

Conjunctions (co-ordinators)

1. Stonecreek is small, *but* Linden is large.

2. Linden is large, *yet* Stonecreek is small.

Adverbs

1. The two cities' governments function *differently*.

2. Stonecreek and Linden handle their respective problems *dissimilarly*.

Prepositions/Prepositional phrases

1. *Unlike* Stonecreek, Linden has many traffic problems.

2. Stonecreek has many traffic problems *in contrast to* Linden.

3. *Instead of* Linden's traffic problems, Stonecreek has calm and quiet streets.

4. Linden is *different from* Stonecreek in its traffic problems.

Transitions

1. Linden is exciting. *On the other hand,* Stonecreek is dull.

2. Stonecreek is dull; *however,* Linden is exciting.

3. Linden is exciting. Stonecreek, *in contrast,* is dull.

NOTE THE USE OF THIS OFTEN MISUSED TRANSITIONAL EXPRESSION:

Stonecreek isn't a big town at all. *On the contrary,* it is quite small.

On the contrary is used to describe a surprising fact—something *contrary* to our expectations—about ONE place.

Showing Similarities

Conjunctions (Co-ordinators)

1. *Both* Stonecreek *and* Linden have much to offer tourists.

2. *Neither* Linden *nor* Stonecreek has a drug problem.

3. *Not only* Linden, *but also* Stonecreek has famous buildings.

Adverbs

1. Their city councils function *identically*.

2. The police departments work *alike*.

Prepositions/Prepositional phrases

1. Stonecreek's town hall is *like* Linden's.

2. Linden is *similar to* Stonecreek in having many tourist attractions.

Transitions

1. Stonecreek has many famous buildings; *likewise*, Linden has much to offer tourists.

2. Linden has a town hall built in 1891. Stonecreek, *similarly*, has a town hall dating from the end of the last century.

3. Stonecreek's inhabitants are very friendly. *In the same way*, the people of Linden are easy to get to know.

Exercise 2

Write in linking words from the lists above in this text. In some of the blanks two or more choices are possible. Use the punctuation marks to help you select an appropriate expression.

Skiing

There are both similarities and differences between waterskiing and downhill snowskiing. First of all, waterskiers use two skis to stand on; *similarly* _____, snowskiers fasten their boots to two long skis. In addition, ____*both*____ waterskiers ____*and*____ snowskiers bend their knees and use their bodies to turn the skis from one side to the other. As a third similarity, waterskiing is ____*like*____ snowskiing in the speed at which it is performed. ____*However*____, the two sports also have some obvious differences. ____*While*____ waterskiing can only take place when it is reasonably warm, snowskiing requires cold weather. Secondly, ____*Unlike*____ a waterskier, a snowskier usually needs two poles for support and control. Another difference lies in the way performers of the sports get their speed. Waterskiers are pulled behind a speedboat on a flat water surface; ____*on the other hand*____, downhill skiers push off from the top of a hill and rely on gravity to make them glide down. The skiers also use their bodies ____*differently*____. ____*Unlike*____ the waterskier, who leans his body backward while holding on to a rope, the downhiller crouches down as far as possible to minimize wind resistance. Finally, a waterskier is evaluated on the basis of style as well as speed, ____*but*____ for a snowskier style is unimportant. Only time counts. As a result, a person who is quite good at one sport may find that the other isn't quite as easy as he or she might have thought.

C. COMMA SPLICES AND RUN-ONS

In addition to fragments, as discussed in Chapter 11, a comma splice is a common punctuation problem. A comma splice means that you have connected two independent clauses with a comma without a co-ordinating conjunction. This is often acceptable in informal writing but should not happen in academic writing. Look at this example of a sentence with a comma splice:

The movie scared me, it had a lot of violence in it.

There are four ways to fix comma splices.

1. You can put a period in the place of the comma and capitalize the beginning of the next sentence.

   The movie scared me. It had a lot of violence in it.

2. You can put a semi-colon in the place of the comma.

   The movie scared me; it had a lot of violence in it.

3. You can insert a co-ordinating conjunction. (See Chapter 12, page 106.)

   The movie scared me, for it had a lot of violence in it.

4. You can make one of the clauses a dependent clause by starting it with a subordinating conjunction.

   The movie scared me because it had a lot of violence in it.

Exercise 3

In the pargraph below, there are four comma splices. Find them and correct them. Try to use each of the four ways above.

Planting Roses

Planting roses is easy if you follow these steps. First you need to measure the diameter of the roots, next you must dig a hole twice as big as that diameter. This hole should be so deep that the roots have plenty of room to grow. Mix some rose fertilizer with the soil at the bottom of the hole, this is to help the rose to flower later. The next step is to form a little hill in the middle of the hole, you are going to spread out the roots over the top of this hill. Hold the rose firmly with one hand and spread out the roots with your other hand. Be careful not to break the roots, they are quite delicate. While you are holding the plant with one hand, pat the soil down gently around the roots. Continue putting soil over the roots until the area around the plant is filled up to a level a little lower than the soil level around it. Finally, water your plant thoroughly. With enough water and some sunshine, you should see your rose plant begin to get leaves in a few weeks.

Another common punctuation problem is run-on sentences. This simply means two or more independent clauses following each other with no punctuation at all. There may also be dependent clauses without appropriate punctuation mixed in with the independent clauses. This situation is harder to correct for two reasons. First of all, you must figure out where one clause ends and another begins. Secondly, there are very many ways to edit the text: you can add (or delete) words and commas, you can add periods and semi-colons, and you can add conjunctions. Look at this example of a run-on sentence and one way of correcting it.

When Janet got home she found out that she had to go shopping because her brother was sick he needed some cold medicine.

CORRECTED:

When Janet got home, she found out that she had to go shopping because her brother was sick. He needed some cold medicine.

Exercise 4

In the text below, there is no punctuation. Try to make sense of it by adding punctuation and capital letters.

Two hours later a mechanic arrived in a big truck he looked like he knew what he was doing because he went right to work under our hood pulled out a couple of wires and said that our car had overheated because our radiator lines were clogged then he went back to his truck he pulled out some tools and rubber tubes in less than fifteen minutes he had our car going again for that work he charged us $50.00 but we didn't mind because we were in a hurry.

D. YOU'RE IN CHARGE: WRITING TO COMMUNICATE

1. You are going to write an essay together with a classmate. Follow this procedure:

   a. Start thinking: what do you two have in common?

   _____

   _____

   _____

   _____

   _____

   _____

b. What are your major differences?

_____

_____

_____

_____

_____

_____

c. Think about situations that are or have been examples of each of the points you listed above. Write them here in outline form.

SIMILARITIES

1. _____

    Ex: _____

    Ex: _____

2. _____

    Ex: _____

    Ex: _____

3. _____

    Ex: _____

    Ex: _____

DIFFERENCES

1. _____

    Ex: _____

    Ex: _____

2. _____

    Ex: _____

    Ex: _____

3. _____

    Ex: _____

    Ex: _____

d. Do your differences outweigh your similarities or vice versa? Write a thesis statement based on your answer to this question.

e. Can you think of a good anecdote as an introduction to this essay?

f. Write your essay together following your outline. Use third person (he/she) when writing your essay.

2. Album covers have become a form of art in the world of popular music. Below are two examples of album covers that have obvious similarities in their content but subtle differences in the message behind the design. With a partner or in a small group, brainstorm about these similarities and differences.

Artist: Supertramp, a pop/rock group from England who had a small but loyal following when they became well-known throughout the world in 1979.

Album: *Even in the Quietest Moments* was released in 1977 and had moderate success.

Artist: Elton John, a piano player/singer/songwriter from England who is well-known for his eccentric performances and clothes, especially hats and glasses.

Album: *Here and There* was recorded live in London and New York in 1974, but the album wasn't released until 1976.

Based on your notes from your discussion, write an essay comparing and/or contrasting these two albums.

E. PEER HELP WORKSHEET

With this Peer Help Worksheet, take the time to offer your classmate specific examples to improve the content of his/her essay. Also, if the organizational pattern isn't clear, help your classmate choose an appropriate pattern from the three choices presented in this chapter.

1. *What did you particularly like about this essay?*

2. *Content*

   In the space below suggest any additional examples or other changes the author might want to make when revising the essay.

3. *Organization*

   a. *What kind of introduction is used in this essay?*

   _____

   b. *Copy the thesis statement here:* _____

   _____

   c. *Does the essay have mostly differences* _____ *or mostly similarities* _____ *?*   (Check one.)

   d. *How many body paragraphs are there?* _____

   e. *What kind of organization is used?*   (Check one.)

   Point by point _____

   Block #1   _____

   Block #2   _____

   Unclear   _____

   f. *What kind of conclusion is used?*   (Check one.)

   Restatement of thesis   _____

   Summary of main points _____

   Extension of thesis   _____

   Other   _____

4. *Editing*

   a. *Check the grammar and punctuation of each of the transitions. Underline anything you think may be incorrect.*

   b. *Check the essay for agreement of subjects and verbs. Draw a line between every subject and verb that you think is incorrect.*

F. OTHER ESSAYS

Do you remember how strange everything seemed when you first arrived in this country? You probably did a lot of comparing in your mind of the people, the customs, and the way of life here and in your home country. When we do our comparing or contrasting in writing, however, we need to make sure that the organizational pattern is clear. Otherwise, the essay may end up being very difficult to read. After you have jotted down notes from brainstorming or freewriting for the suggested essays below, choose an organizational pattern and write out your notes in that pattern. Pay particular attention to the thesis statement; it must match the essays which follow.

1. Your mother or father probably led quite different lives in their youth than you do now. Write an essay comparing the two lifestyles. For example, consider these points:

    a. In what kind of a house did he/she live compared to the one you live in today?

    b. Did he/she study or work at your age?

    c. What was his/her attitude toward freedom of choice compared to yours?

    d. What were his/her values compared to yours?

2. You have probably read many novels in your lifetime, in your native language and perhaps also in English. Pick two books and compare and/or contrast them. Consider the following points:

    a. How were the main characters similar or different?

    b. What did the stories (the plots) of the two books have in common? How were they different?

3. Think about the city or area you live in now. One obvious difference from your home town is that everybody here speaks another language than yours. However, can you compare your home town with your current place of residence in other ways? Think about these points:

    a. Are the houses/apartments similar or different?

    b. Can you compare the roads and traffic patterns?

    c. How do the parks and open areas compare with those of your country? Are the trees and plants similar or different? Do people use these areas in the same way?

14 Exemplification

A. MODEL ESSAYS

Read the two models carefully.

Model 1

The American Experience

To an international student, the United States often seems to be a collection of ''countries'' that have little in common. There is a rural, midwestern ''country'' with huge, flat prairies and a few small towns here and there, the big city ''country'' of New York City, Los Angeles, or Houston, the suburban ''country'' with its subdivisions that spread out forever, and so on. Visitors often wonder if there is anything at all that unites people in these diverse areas and makes them all Americans. While they have not become one single culture, the people in the U.S. still have some shared experiences that shape them and make them all one people.

The primary shared experience is high school. While 12% of students from 14 to 18 attend private schools for part of their school years, the majority goes to free public schools. In general, the grade level requirements are similar all over the U.S. This means that a tenth grade student in Topeka, Kansas will, by the end of the year, have learned basically the same as his fellow student in Yakima, Washington. In addition to the regular classroom work, the high school experience includes extracurricular activities which are considered equally important in all corners of this country. Language clubs, debating clubs, and participation in sports are all considered almost as valuable as textbook study in making the children civilized members of society. School sports are particularly important. Being on a team or supporting it from the seats develops ''school spirit'' and creates an identification with the school for the students. Anyone who has gone through American high school has been ''Americanized'' in this way.

The second unifying factor is television. Americans are a television-watching and television influenced people. In 1981 each family with a T.V. set in this country watched it an average of almost 7 hours a day! With three major networks, an extensive public TV system, and a growing number of cable channels, there is always something on for everyone. Different age and social groups watch similar programs, and these form another shared experience. No matter where you live or how much money you have, Johnny Carson appears on your set every evening. The same can be said for the situation comedies, the soap operas, and the news. TV is great at giving shared experiences.

Finally, consider the importance of the automobile on American life. Americans like to travel, mostly by car. Countless songs have been written about the romance of "movin' on," going somewhere else, being "on the road." The car makes Americans a mobile people both in terms of traveling and in changing residences. The average American family moves every five years. Such a constant mixing of the population means that more people in this country meet new people and make new friends than in any other country. The need to change the background scenery becomes a basic ingredient in the American soul.

In conclusion, although the "melting pot" view of the United States does not seem to be accurate, Americans do indeed have a lot in common. As a result, if you can't think of anything to say to a person you meet in this country, try asking him about his high school, his opinion of a current TV show, or his preference in cars. You're sure to get a lively discussion!

VOCABULARY
prairies = plains, flat areas of land
extracurricular = outside of regular classes
mobile = having the ability to move
accurate = correct

Model 2

Our Airways are Unsafe

In 1982, President Ronald Reagan put into effect a program of airline deregulation which had been introduced under the Carter administration. This new law allowed airlines to set their prices as low as they wanted and to offer flights as often as they wanted. In some ways, the program has been a success: ticket prices have indeed gone down, and there are more flights to popular cities than ever before. However, deregulation has also been one of the causes of our current problem of air travel safety. While 1986 had the fewest air travel deaths of any previous year, it was still a year which saw a sharply increasing number of *near* crashes, and 1987 was even worse. Due to more pilot errors, fewer controllers on the ground, and poor maintenance of airplanes, our airways are more dangerous now than they have ever been.

The number of pilot errors which lead to near crashes is increasing at an alarming rate. One example of pilot error happened on July 8, 1987, when a Delta Airlines jumbo jet found itself within 100 feet of another plane. Delta Airlines, usually considered to be one of the industry's most safety-conscious airlines, has had many such near misses. Two separate incidents involving this company occurred on July 19, 1987. Over the state of Virginia, two Delta planes came within 1.3 miles of one another, and on the same day the captain of a Delta Boeing 737 had to change his course quickly to avoid a small, private plane that came as close as 1,300 feet to the jet. Moreover, on that same day a small commuter plane which followed a large jet too closely was bounced about by the 747's exhaust turbulence and fell to within 100 feet of the ground before the pilot could regain control of the aircraft. *All* of these near accidents could have been avoided.

A second cause of near collisions is the lack of properly trained air traffic controllers. In 1981 the controllers went on strike for higher pay and better working conditions, and President Reagan fired all of them. Even now, the airports still don't have enough controllers and must deal with controllers with very little experience. Examples of near misses due to controller failure, such as the close encounter of a PanAm jet and a Venezuelan plane in July, 1987, are numerous. The PanAm plane had received permission to climb to 2,000 feet, but the controller didn't realize that there was another plane also at that altitude. The two planes missed each other by 800 feet. In that same month in Boston, two airplanes were given permission to take off on crossing runways. The collision was avoided when the tower realized what was happening and ordered the USAir aircraft to stop before it taxied right into the path of the Delta flight under full power. The airplane taking off had no way to change its course at that point. It was a very close call. A third example can be seen in the case of a United Airlines flight coming into O'Hare airport in Chicago on July 19, 1987. This plane had to stop its attempt to land near the airport when the pilot noticed six Air Force F-16s in the process of touching down on a crossing runway. The Air Force planes had also been cleared for landing by the controllers at O'Hare. With so many planes to keep an eye on, it is not surprising that air traffic controllers make mistakes at times.

A third cause of near accidents is poor maintenance of airplanes due to the airlines' interest in cutting costs. In February 1987, a mechanic working on a Continental Airlines jet told the plane's crew to wait while he went to get some parts. When he returned a few minutes later, the airplane was gone! It had taken off with one of the fuselage doors still hanging open. The plane was ordered to return to the airport, and it landed safely. This could have been a great disaster. In the same year, Eastern Airlines was ordered to pay more than $9.5 million in fines for over 78,000 maintenance violations. Maintenance is costly and time-consuming but absolutely necessary.

In conclusion, our airways *are* unsafe. Should all these examples then make you take the train next time you travel? A better way would be to put pressure on government officials to establish rules for pilot training, the number of hours in the air for the crew, the number of flights taking off and landing at any given time, air controller education and training, and procedures for maintenance. With stricter regulations, most of the problems would be solved.

VOCABULARY
deregulation = taking rules away
controllers = the people in the tower at an airport who direct planes while
     taking off and landing
maintenance = keeping something in good working order

wing flaps = the small parts of an airplane's wings which move up and down
a jumbo jet = a big airplane
a commuter plane = a small airplane that people can take to work
exhaust turbulence = the force of air behind a plane
to lack = not to have something
to taxi = to drive an airplane on the ground
to cut costs = to make something cost less money
fuselage = the body of a plane
close call = an accident that almost happens

Obviously, both of the model essays in this chapter are quite long, much longer than those of previous chapters. When you are using examples to support an opinion, you need to make sure that your reader is convinced. In Model 1, the author had only *three* examples (high school, TV, and cars), but all three of these were long and well-developed. In Model 2, the author chose instead to give *several* examples for each of the three main points. Naturally, you are not expected to write essays as long as these models, but you do need to ask yourself: "Have I given enough clear examples to convince my reader?"

Exercise 1

Below are four thesis statements and lists of possible examples to support them. Put a check mark next to those that you would include in an essay with that thesis statement and be prepared to explain *why* you chose those.

1. Thesis: Sports can cause injury.

    _____ Basketball develops team spirit.
    _____ Runners often injure their knees.
    _____ "Tennis elbow" is painful.
    _____ Surfing gives you great balance.
    _____ Swimming makes girls broad-shouldered.
    _____ Skiing is an exciting sport.
    _____ Skiers with a leg cast is a common sight.

2. Thesis: Air pollution is a growing problem.

    _____ Pollution from the U.S. makes acid rain fall in Canada.
    _____ Car exhaust is poisonous, and there is an increasing number of cars on the road.
    _____ Smokers pollute our indoor environment, but there are fewer smokers than before.
    _____ We should convert to nuclear energy.
    _____ New plants can be developed that can stand the levels of pollution.
    _____ 80% of our planet's surface is covered with water.
    _____ Switzerland is losing trees at an alarming rate due to polluted air.

3. Thesis: The Civil War was mostly caused by economic differences in the South and the North.

_____ The South was agricultural while the North was industrial.
_____ Abraham Lincoln opposed slavery.
_____ The war lasted from 1860 to 1865, with great losses on both sides.
_____ The South felt it needed slaves to maintain its economy.
_____ The living conditions for the factory workers of the North were just as bad as those for the slaves in the South.
_____ The economy in the North was based on manufacturing and needed less manpower.

4. Thesis: Community colleges are better for freshmen than universities.

_____ A university has an excellent academic reputation.
_____ Classes are smaller in a community college.
_____ I prefer community colleges.
_____ You can get a loan to pay tuition at a university.
_____ Community colleges are cheaper than universities.
_____ At a university you often have an assistant as a teacher, not the professor.
_____ A university has a large library.
_____ You can take the same classes at a community college as at a university.
_____ Many students transfer from a community college to a university after two years.

Exercise 2

Below are three thesis statements for example essays. In groups of three or four, discuss possible examples you can use to support the theses. Write down the three best examples for each and present them to the class with your reasons for choosing them.

1. Today's music is exciting.

   _____

   _____

   _____

2. Having a pet makes your life richer.

   _____

   _____

   _____

3. Many countries have big city traffic problems.

   _____

   _____

   _____

Exercise 3

There are many ways to organize your examples for an essay. Most example essays tend to use a "least to most important" pattern of organization. Below are two thesis statements and three lists of examples for each. Which one is organized according to the "least to most important" pattern? Discuss the lists in small groups, and be prepared to give reasons for your choice. Many answers may be possible.

I. Thesis statement: The quality of modern life is decreasing due to noise pollution.

  A. 1. home computers making an irritating noise
        2. telephones ringing all the time
        3. modern music louder than ever
        4. more factories—more production—more noise
        5. more cars/planes/trains—more noise

  B. 1. more cars/planes/trains—more noise
        2. more factories—more production—more noise
        3. modern music louder than ever
        4. telephones ringing all the time
        5. home computers making an irritating noise

  C. 1. telephones ringing all the time
        2. more cars/planes/trains—more noise
        3. home computers making an irritating noise
        4. more factories—more production—more noise
        5. modern music—louder than ever

II. Thesis statement: Construction work in Southern California can be a satisfying job.

  A. 1. get a feeling of "making a mark"
        2. see a project from beginning to end
        3. friendship with fellow workers
        4. get a good physical workout
        5. get a nice tan from being outside all day

  B. 1. get a nice tan from being outside all day
        2. get a good physical workout
        3. friendship with fellow workers
        4. getting a feeling of "making a mark"
        5. see a project from beginning to end

  C. 1. friendship with fellow workers
        2. see a project from beginning to end
        3. get a good physical workout
        4. get a nice tan from working outside all day
        5. get a feeling of "making a mark"

B. LINKING WORDS

As with all other essay types previously discussed, example essays also need linking words (conjunctions, adverbs, prepositions, and transitions). Some of the most common linking words are listed below.

Explanation

> in this case
> in other words
> that is

1. A runner may be injuring herself without even knowing it. *In this case*, a small pain can grow into a serious disability.

2. Air pollution, *that is*, unhealthy air, is a problem for everyone.

Emphasis

> indeed
> in fact

1. There are many examples supporting this claim. *Indeed*, the list is so long that I can only pick out a few of them at this time.

2. Tony is an example of an extremely patient person; *in fact*, I sometimes think that he doesn't notice the time passing.

Causation

> due to
> because
> since

1. *Due to* the North's industrial economy, it was able to change rapidly.

2. The noise made by telephones is important *since* it has an increasingly elevated position in our lives.

Consequence

> therefore
> as a result
> consequently
> hence

1. Anna is a very friendly person; *therefore/as a result/consequently/hence/*, she is one of my best friends.

Opposition

in spite of
despite
even though
although

1. *In spite of/Despite* the poor attendance at the concert, we thoroughly enjoyed ourselves.

2. *Even though* he is wealthy, he never spends a penny on anyone else.

3. *Although/Though* it may rain, we'll go anyway.

Continuation

in addition
furthermore
in addition to
also

1. *Newsweek* is a very popular weekly news magazine. *In addition/Furthermore, Time* is a news magazine read by many people every week.

2. *In addition to the Atlantic, U.S. News and World Report* usually contains excellent reporting.

3. *The National Enquirer* is inappropriate for academic use. *Star* is *also* inappropriate in this regard.

Conclusion

in conclusion
to sum up

1. *In conclusion*, we can see that the four factors mentioned above have greatly influenced South African life.

2. *To sum up*, there are three main reasons for poverty: lack of education, lack of opportunity, and lack of a support system.

✓ Exercise 4

Here is an essay with blanks for linking words. Read the whole essay through first, and then insert the linking words you think would fit best in the blanks. Use the punctuation marks to help you pick appropriate words/phrases. Note that transitions can sometimes come in the middle of a sentence with commas on either side of them.

Choose from the linking words below. You may use the same one several times. You will not need all of them.

first	for example	because of	indeed	therefore
second	for instance	in other words	in fact	as a result
third	such as	due to	consequently	next
in conclusion	that is	because	despite	in addition
finally	even though	since	also	however

Gridlock in L.A.

Yesterday I wanted to go downtown to buy some books. My classes end at 2:30 P.M., so there was no way that I could leave earlier. It is only 15 miles from school to the downtown area, but it took me 45 minutes! Finding a parking place near the bookstore took another 20 minutes. Getting my books was a breeze; I probably only spent half an hour in the store before I had found what I wanted, but the return journey was as awful as the first drive. I waited in a line of about 50 cars to get on the freeway, and once I was on, the traffic came to a complete standstill. I didn't get home until 5 P.M. The traffic situation in Los Angeles is terrible.

_____First_____, the streets are too narrow for the amount of traffic they handle. Interstate 5, _____for example_____, has only two lanes in certain areas, and the 5 and 405 interchange is especially awful. _____Consequently_____, during rush hours, you may have to wait as long as 15 minutes just to move a few hundred yards. _____In addition_____ to these two roads, Interstate 101 is also a headache. It goes right through the heart of downtown, and, _____as a result_____, it is a central route for many people who live in the L.A. area. _____Because +_____ it is an older road, it was not built for today's heavy traffic, and it is jammed, _____that is_____, filled with cars, almost all day. The Long Beach freeway, the 605, is _____also_____ a serious problem. Many people who moved out of Los Angeles to Long Beach to get away from traffic jams and noise have found that they haven't escaped after all. _____Since +_____ these people need to get downtown to go to work, they have no other choice than to use the 605. _____Therefore_____, the 605 is a virtual parking lot from 7 to 10 A.M. and again from 3 to 7 P.M.

_____Next / Second_____, there is not enough public transportation _____such as_____ taxis, buses, or trains. _____In fact / Consequently_____, while you might find a taxi at one of the airports, you will never see them anywhere else. The distances in the L.A. area are just too great, and taking a taxi would be too expensive for most people. There are, _____however_____, a few buses, but _____due to_____ the spread-out nature of Southern Californian development, these buses do not help the situation much. They don't run often enough, and, _____in addition_____, they get caught in traffic jams. Another example of poor public transportation is our lack of trains. Between Santa Ana and Los Angeles, _____in fact_____, there are only four trains every day. How can commuters travel to and from their jobs by train if there are never trains that run when they need them? Public transportation is _____indeed / therefore_____ a problem in Los Angeles.

_____Finally_____, the residents of the area simply don't seem to care very much about the situation. One solution, _____for instance_____, could be for workers in the same business to carpool, _in other words_____, to agree to ride to work together in the same car or van. _Even though_____ as many as 50 or more employees may live in the same area and work at the same place, they don't often decide to carpool. _In addition_____, they have gotten so used to their cars that driving even for short distances has become a habit. Instead of actively trying to solve a common problem, most people appear to ignore it, except by complaining when they get stuck in freeway traffic jams. _Consequently/Therefore/As a result_____, nothing very much gets done.

_In conclusion_____, the traffic in the Los Angeles area is certainly a mess. It has even introduced a new vocabulary item into the English language: gridlock, _that is_____, having so many cars on the road that no one can go anywhere. One of these days total gridlock will occur in L.A., and when it does, there is nothing we can do but get out of our cars and start to walk. That will be an interesting sight.

C. YOU'RE IN CHARGE: WRITING TO COMMUNICATE

1. You are going to write an essay about the transportation situation in either your capital city, or the city or town you live in now. Start getting ideas by discussing these questions in a small group:

   a. Is it easy or difficult to get around in this town?

   b. How long does it take you to get to and from school?

   c. How easy or difficult is it for you to get to and from an evening movie?

   d. What do you think of the bus system in this town?

   e. Are there any trains or subways? If there are, are they good?

   f. How easy or difficult is it for you to go shopping (clothes, food, books, etc.)?

Take notes on the discussion. The information you get from the others will help you with examples for the following essay.

   Now that you have some ideas and examples to use in an essay, it is time to plan your own. Make a brief outline and write your essay. Don't forget to write a clear thesis statement including a controlling idea.

2. Below are five essay topic areas. Decide which one interests you the most and put a checkmark next to it.

   1. Personalities
   2. The ideal man/woman
   3. Movies
   4. Animals as pets
   5. Housing

Your teacher will divide the class into five groups. (If there are fewer than 15 or more than 25 students, the teacher will select the topics.) In your group, discuss possible controlling ideas to make the topics into thesis statements, and try to come up with as many examples as you can in support of the thesis statement that you make. Use the suggestions below for each group as a starting point to develop examples. When your discussion is over, write an outline for your essay.

Group 1

Are you *shy* or *outgoing*? Discuss how a shy/outgoing person would behave in these situations:

a. when she meets new people
b. when she is called on in class
c. when she is unhappy with her living situation
d. when she has to call a stranger on the phone
e. other situations?

Group 2

What is your idea of the ideal man/woman? For example, you may decide that he/she should be an optimistic person. Discuss examples of how an optimistic person acts.

Here are some adjectives you might use:

graceful, strong, rich, beautiful/handsome, tall, short, quiet, cheerful, funny, warm, hard-working, intelligent, friendly, etc.

Group 3

What is the best movie that you have ever seen? Why was it so good? What is the worst movie that you have ever seen? Why? In this group, try to find specific examples of what a GOOD or BAD movie is.

Good movies:

_____

_____

_____

_____

Bad movies:

_____

_____

_____

_____

What do the good movies have in common? What characteristics make them good? Similarly, what characteristics make the bad movies bad?

Group 4

Is a dog "man's best friend?" Discuss examples of dog behavior that show that it is (or isn't) good for people to have dogs as pets.

Group 5

What is the housing situation in the place where you live now? Is it good, bad, or adequate? Is it expensive or cheap? Are the houses well built? Are they big or small? After discussing what the housing situation is like, try to find as many examples as possible to support your opinion.

Now write your essay following your outline.

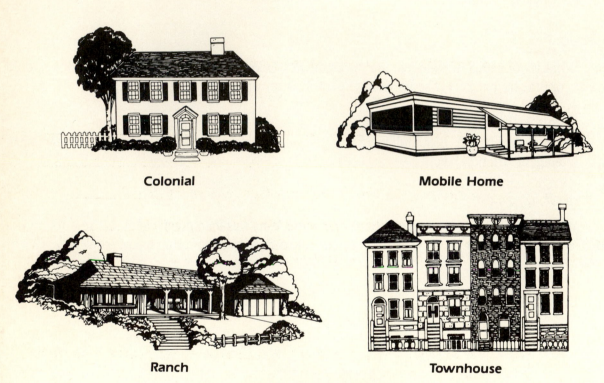

Colonial   Mobile Home

Ranch   Townhouse

Apartment/Dormitory

D. PEER HELP WORKSHEET

Here's this chapter's Peer Help Worksheet. Be sure to help your classmate add specific examples if this is necessary to better support the thesis statement.

1. *What did you like about the ideas presented in this essay?*

2. *Content*

   If you have any suggestions for improving the content of this essay, write them here.

3. *Organization*

   a. *Write the thesis of the essay here:*

   _____

   _____

   b. *How many examples are there that support the thesis?* _____

   c. *Do you think the writer should add more examples?* _____

   If yes, give some suggestions here:

   d. *Is there a conclusion?* _____

   If you have any suggestions for changes in the conclusion, write them here:

4. *Editing*

   a. *Check the essay for the use of articles. Circle any that you think are incorrect, and add a circle anywhere you think there should be an additional article.*

   b. *Check the essay for punctuation used with linking words.*

   c. *Check the essay for spelling. Underline all words you think are misspelled.*

E. OTHER ESSAYS

As you have seen in this chapter, essays that use examples are those where your opinion on a subject forms the thesis statement, and the examples you use support that opinion to convince the reader. When you write essays like these later in your career, you will probably be expected to do research and use other writers' opinions and examples. However, at this level, you are only expected to use your own examples. Below are three suggestions for essays supported by examples.

1. Every country has problems. In your opinion, what are the major problems that your country faces? Are they economic, social, political, or something else? Write an essay with detailed examples.

2. If you have watched television in this country at all, you must have seen quite a few commercials. What is your opinion of the way commercials are used in the U.S.? Do you think they are useful or not useful for the amount and type of TV programming we have here? Are they good or bad? Write an essay supporting your opinion.

3. We all have to eat to stay alive. Every country has its own type of food, and the United States is no different. What do you think of American food? Support your essay with concrete examples.

Appendices

Appendix 1: Punctuation

A. COMMAS AND SEMI-COLONS

There are certain generally accepted rules of punctuation for academic writing. By punctuation, we mean periods, commas, and semi-colons. Below, you will find rules for use of these punctuation marks followed by two exercises.

IC = INDEPENDENT CLAUSE
AC = ADVERBIAL DEPENDENT CLAUSE
X   = WORD or PHRASE

Rule 1

You put a comma after a word, phrase, or adverbial clause preceding the subject of the independent clause.

1. _____ X/AC_____, _____ IC_____.

   EX.: Jonas is very shy. *However,* Andy is quite outgoing.

   EX.: Jonas is very shy. *For this reason,* he never goes to parties.

   EX.: *Because Jonas is very shy,* he never goes to parties.

   Exceptions:

   a) Co-ordinating conjunctions are not followed by commas.

   EX.: Jonas is very shy, so he never goes to parties.

   b) Sometimes, one-word time phrases are not followed by commas.

   EX.: Jonas took a long shower. Then he got dressed.

Rule 2

Two independent clauses which are closely connected in meaning may be connected with a semi-colon. In addition, transitions joining two independent clauses may be preceded by a semi-colon and followed by a comma.

2. _____ IC_____; _____ IC_____.

   _____ IC_____; transition, _____ IC_____.

   EX.: Jonas is very shy; he never goes to parties.

   EX.: Jonas is very shy; *therefore,* he never goes to parties.

Rule 3

When an adverbial clause follows an independent clause, there is no comma following the independent clause.

3. _____IC_____ _____AC_____.

    EX.: Jonas never goes to parties *because he is very shy*.

Rule 4

When a co-ordinating conjunction connects two independent clauses, a comma precedes the conjunction.

4. _____IC_____, co-ordinating conjunction _____IC_____.

    EX.: Jonas is very shy, so he never goes to parties.

    (Note: See "exceptions", rule 1.)

Rule 5

Three or more items in a list are separated by commas.

5. _____X, X, and X_____ .

    EX.: We had meat, potatoes, and corn for dinner.

    EX.: Tom went to the University of Illinois because he liked the climate, admired its professors, and thought highly of its medical school.

Exercise 1

In the paragraph below, add commas and semi-colons where they are needed and delete those that are wrong.

> Three main events caused Daniel to regret that he had bought a used car. First of all he noticed that the tires were a lot worse than the salesman had promised him. One day when it was raining he almost had an accident, because he couldn't stop fast enough consequently he had to go out and buy a new set of tires. Since he needed to save money; he was quite upset about this. The following day he saw a pool of oil underneath the car, and found out, that it had a serious oil leak. That cost him a pretty penny too. The final irritation occurred at the service station while the mechanic was fixing the oil leak. He discovered that the odometer had been turned back! It read 57,000 miles but the car had probably gone at least 100,000. Daniel now says that the most expensive thing in the world to buy is a used car.

B. SPECIAL PROBLEMS

Both native and non-native writers of English have trouble with certain rules of punctuation. The three basic problems are called fragments, comma splices, and run-on sentences. Look below for explanations of these terms.

Fragments

A fragment is a phrase or a part of a sentence which is incomplete. The minimum sentence in English must contain a subject and a verb with a tense. (Imperatives are special cases.) Three common fragment problems are:

a) a phrase without a subject
   EX.: Went to the store yesterday.

b) a phrase without a verb with a tense
   EX.: John going to the store.

c) a dependent clause
   EX.: Because it was hot.

These fragment problems can be solved in the following ways:

a) add a subject
   EX.: *I* went to the store yesterday.

b) change the verb form to include a tense
   EX.: John *was going* to the store.

c) attach the dependent clause to an independent clause
   EX.: *We went to the beach* because it was hot.
                    OR
   EX.: Because it was hot, *we went to the beach.*

Comma Splices

A comma splice means the connection of two independent clauses with a comma. Below is an example of this mistake:

   EX.: I went to my friend's house, he wasn't home.

This mistake can be fixed in the following ways:

a) substitute a period for the comma
   EX.: I went to my friend's house. He wasn't home.

b) substitute a semi-colon for the comma
   EX.: I went to my friend's house; he wasn't home.

c) add a co-ordinating conjunction
   EX.: I went to my friend's house, but he wasn't home.

d) add a transition with the appropriate punctuation
   EX.: I went to my friend's house; however, he wasn't home.

Run-On Sentences

A run-on sentence is one in which you have included more than one independent clause (plus possible dependent clauses) without punctuation. These can be very difficult to make sense of, but you must try to separate the run-on into its independent and dependent clauses, and punctuate according to the chart in Part A. Below is an example of a run-on sentence:

> EX.: I didn't have enough milk in the house yesterday so I went to the store to buy some the store was closed so I drove to my friend's house but he wasn't at home I decided not to eat breakfast.

By adding commas and periods, we get:

> EX.: I didn't have enough milk in the house yesterday, so I went to the store to buy some. The store was closed, so I drove to my friend's house, but he wasn't at home. I decided not to eat breakfast.

In addition to these rules and suggestions, please see punctuation rules in Chapter 11, pages 87 and 90, Chapter 12, pages 106-107, and Chapter 13, pages 121-122.

Exercise

Solve these punctuation problems by following the suggestions above.

Fragments

1. I loved Hawaii. Because the water was warm. We went swimming every day.

2. I have never been so scared in my life. The following day. We decided to leave.

3. There are many sports I enjoy. Playing soccer. Tennis. Even skiing.

4. After we pitched our tents. We ate dinner. And we went to bed.

Comma Splices

1. There are many types of dogs, I especially like hunting dogs.

2. The day after it began to rain, it rained so hard that we had to stay inside, to go out would have been impossible.

3. I'll never forget my first day in Alaska, because the temperature was 20 degrees below zero, we had to wear every piece of clothing we owned.

Run-Ons

1. I have ridden on a roller coaster many times since but nothing can be compared to that first time it was a terrifying experience even though it was over in less than five minutes.

2. Nuclear power is a controversial issue in the United States today some people argue that it is a much cleaner source of power than coal or oil but others are afraid of the possible dangers.

Appendix 2: Summary of Linking Words Focused On In This Text

	Transitions	Conjunctions Subordinate	Conjunctions Coordinate	Prepositions	Adverbs	Other
Chronology	first, etc. at first next after that later on finally then	after before while when	and or	after before since prior to	immediately constantly now	
Description				to the left to the right on both sides next to on front of behind on top of under above on/at the end		
Example	for example for instance					another example is
Causation		because since	for	due to		

Consequence	therefore
	for this
	  reason
	as a result/
	  consequence
	consequently
	hence
			so			

Opposition		even though although		in spite of despite		
Difference	on the other hand however in contrast	whereas while	but yet	unlike in contrast to instead of different from	differently	
Similarity	likewise similarly in the same way		both...and neither...nor not only...but also	like similar to	alike	
Explanation	in this case in other words that is					
Emphasis	indeed in fact					
Continuation	in addition furthermore			in addition to	also	
Conclusion	in conclusion to sum up					

Appendix 3:
A General Peer Help Worksheet

1. *What do you like best about this essay?*

2. *Content*

   a. *What is the rhetorical pattern used in this essay?*

   b. *Do the individual paragraphs have unity? Underline sentences you think are irrelevant.*

3. *Organization*

   a. *What kind of introductory paragraph does this essay have?* Check one.
      _____ *personal anecdote*
      _____ *third person anecdote*
      _____ *interesting fact or statistic*
      _____ *historical introduction*
      _____ *general to specific*

   b. *Underline the thesis statement. Circle the controlling idea.*

   c. *Do the body paragraphs have good coherence?*

   d. *What type of concluding paragraph does this essay have?* Check one.
      _____ *summary-type*
      _____ *restatement/final comment-type*

4. *Editing*

   a. *Check for problems with fragments, comma splices and run-on sentences.*

   b. *Put "sp" above any words which are misspelled.*

Appendix 4:
Suggested Correction Symbols

cap	Mistake in use of capital letter(s)
p	Mistake in punctuation (i.e., commas, semi-colons, periods, etc.)
¶	Mistake in paragraph format
sp	Spelling mistake
ref	Unclear reference of pronoun
ww	Wrong word
wf	Wrong form of word
wo	Wrong word order
t	Mistake in verb tense and/or aspect
voc	Mistake in use of active or passive voice
art	Mistake in article use
prep	Mistake in preposition use
agr	Mistake in agreement of subject and verb
#	Mistake in number (singular/plural)
poss	Mistake in use of possessive form
^	Omission (word(s) missing)
X	Drawn through a word, this indicates that the word should be omitted.
frag	Sentence fragment
rs	Run–on sentence
cs	Comma splice
?	Unclear passage or sentence

Appendix 5:
Paragraph and Essay Evaluation

SCORING		ASPECTS OF GOOD WRITING	
Exceptional: 25-23 Very Good: 22-20 Average: 19-17 Needs Improvement: 16-0 SCORE:		**Content/Ideas**	
		excellent support (interesting to read) unity/completeness relevance to topic assigned	
Exceptional: 25-23 Very Good: 22-20 Average: 19-17 Needs Improvement: 16-0 SCORE:		**Organization**	
		Paragraphs	**Essays**
		topic sentence clear controlling idea body concluding sentence coherence cohesion	introductory paragraph thesis statement with clear controlling idea body: good paragraph organization concluding paragraph coherence/cohesion
Exceptional: 25-23 Very Good: 22-20 Average: 19-17 Needs Improvement: 16-0 SCORE:		**Grammar/Structure**	
		sophistication of sentence structure complex/compound sentences tenses/voice subject/verb agreement articles	
Exceptional: 15-14 Very Good: 13-12 Average: 11-10 Needs Improvement: 9-0 SCORE:		**Words/Word Forms**	
		sophistication of vocabulary items correct idiomatic use of vocabulary items correct word forms	
Exceptional: 10 Very Good: 9-8 Average: 7-6 Needs Improvement: 5-0 SCORE:		**Mechanics**	
		no fragments, run-ons or comma splices spelling commas periods capitalization good paragraph format	
TOTAL SCORE:		**Comments**	

Index